BIRKENHEAD
An Illustrated History

BIRKENHEAD
An Illustrated History

Ralph T. Brocklebank

breedon **books**
PUBLISHING

First published in Great Britain in 2003 by
The Breedon Books Publishing Company Limited
Breedon House, 3 The Parker Centre,
Derby, DE21 4SZ.

ISBN 1 85983 350 0

Printed and bound by Butler & Tanner,
Frome, Somerset, England.

Cover printing by Lawrence-Allen Colour Printers,
Weston-super-Mare, Somerset, England.

CONTENTS

Introduction

Part 1
Earliest Times to 1810 12

Part 2.
Development and Government-Funded Plan
The town 1810 – 1870 27

Part 3
Exploitation to 1900 50

Part 4
Light and Dark. Wealth and Poverty, Edwardian Period to 1914
Sounds and Alarms 73

Part 5
Charity and Social Improvement. Art and Education.
Graham White and the Liberals up to 1939 93

Part 6
War, Tragedy, Dock Strikes, Glorious Moments to 1974 123

Part 7
The Race to Improve the town and Raise its Profile from 1974 to Date 150

Bibliography 166

Index 167

Dedicated to Brenda

ACKNOWLEDGEMENTS

For their unstinting help and encouragement
my thanks are due to all my friends at
Birkenhead Library, especially the
information services ladies and gentlemen.

Birkenhead – the name is associated
with ships, industry, dark days,
stormy waters, a damp climate and
the consequent slurred catarrhal
dialect special to the town.

BURKINED falls dull and heavy on
the ear. Frank Field's pronunciation is
lilting. Freddie Starr's version is
native dockers' diction. Sitcom's
Hyacinth Bucket 'poshifies' the name.
Take your choice! It's cool to say
Berstyered.

INTRODUCTION

I attended school in Bebington, of green beauty and ancient history, in 1953. Although I visited neighbouring Birkenhead on my way to Liverpool or for essential shopping trips at that time, I paid little attention to the town and its buildings.

The 1950s were dull and dreary due to hardship, grime-ridden bomb damage and the continuing shortages of the late war. Ruined by the blitz, Birkenhead was a place to avoid and from which one would 'avert one's eyes'. I was blind, I was ignorant, I was arrogant. Until... I attended a Sixth Form Cultural Lecture in May 1953. The Town Clerk of Birkenhead came to my school and told the story of Birkenhead.

The Danish settlers entered the hall, the Romans built a bridge close by, the Black Monks chanted amongst sacred Priory ruins. Kings and courtiers, Cavaliers and Roundheads thronged the aisles of the school hall. Outside, the Woodside Ferry brought men of wealth to the Birkenhead shores. A silver town was conceived on a grand plan filled with palatial buildings and busy docks, quays and new imaginative roads, transport and railways.

This transformation scene in my head on that day was 'Birkenhead'. For some reason, a chart of James Gillespie Graham's 'Revolutionary Gridiron Plan', which was displayed at the lecture, has stayed in my mind ever since. The clarity and simplicity of the plan coloured my view of Birkenhead from that time. I began to look at the town with interest and enquiry.

Who built the Birkenhead Priory? Why was there a decline in the town's fortunes in the 1870s? What prompted rioting and strikes in Birkenhead?

When I was invited to try my hand at penning this history, my mind was already prepared for the task. I only hope that my words are adequate to the greatness of the subject.

Ralph T. Brocklebank
October 2003

Part 1
EARLIEST
TIMES TO 1810

IN THIS, the 21st century, it is hard to imagine Birkenhead as it might have been 2,000 years ago. The River Birket has flowed out into the Mersey here since before the time Man the Cultivator appeared, some 5,000 years ago. He settled in the Birket's heavily-wooded valley, leaving flint axe-heads and sickles behind him for subsequent generations to uncover.

The Romans arrived in about AD 59. They left their mark on Birkenhead by building a bridge – possibly part of the road to the Roman port and settlement at Meols and the High Lake (Hoylake). Foundations of the Roman Bridge were discovered in 1850 during excavations for the building of a railway bridge at Bridge Street.

It is logical to assume from the name Birkenhead that this was always a place of great natural beauty. A promontory surrounded on three sides by a river abounding in fish. A headland crowned with birch trees where a squirrel might flit from tree to tree. Here was a haven for those seeking refuge, amongst them the early invading Scandinavian settlers of the 10th century. They named their new home Bierce Heved (headland of birch trees) using Old English and Scandinavian words to describe the distinguishing landmarks.

Thereafter invasions, intrusions and settlements ebbed and flowed around the promontory like Mother Mersey, until a strong, new force entered the kingdom of England. William the Conqueror and his earls vanquished the Anglo Saxons and took control after the invasion of 1066.

Cheshire became an earldome under Ranulph II and barons were created to maintain orderly regions of the county. William's land inventory of 1097 – *Domesday Book* – makes no reference to Birkenhead, however.

Then in 1150 the third Baron Hamo Mascy had governance of Dunham and lands and estates of

A Roman bridge discovered in 1850 during the building of the railway bridge at Bridge End.

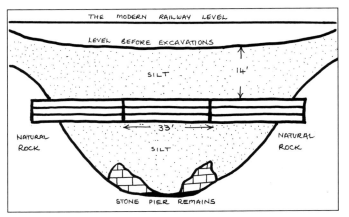

THE MODERN RAILWAY LEVEL

LEVEL BEFORE EXCAVATIONS

SILT   14'

NATURAL ROCK   NATURAL ROCK

33'

SILT

STONE PIER REMAINS

Wirral including the tiny peasant community of Birkenhead. 'Bierce Heved' was at the time a ferry point across to Liverpool at the safest passage of the Mersey.

Hamo Mascy, in the manner of his wealthy Norman contemporaries, was a devout Roman Catholic who sought divine favour for his own soul and the soul of his family. To that end he financed the foundation of a Benedictine Priory at Birkenhead.

Building commenced in about 1150 during the reign of Stephen. The Priory housed 16 monks led by their Prior. Appropriately the establishment was dedicated to and named after St James the Great – the patron saint of pilgrims.

The Benedictine Order of monks is required by their rule to succour the traveller and the wayfaring stranger as though catering for the Saviour himself. The Order is also responsible for the care and maintenance of ferries, roads and bridges. What better site for such a holy house? Birkenhead was on the route of travellers moving up and down the country from North to South.

Many of these were pilgrims journeying to the shrine of St Werburgh in Chester. Theirs was a hazardous journey in both directions: roads were in poor condition; there was danger of theft and even murder from cut-purses and footpads; and there was a fast and furious river to cross in fragile ferry boats. Birkenhead Priory's band of brothers provided rest, refreshment and divine protection on a long and exhausting sacred journey.

Prior's gate, Birkenhead Priory.

The Prior had responsibility to God, to the Pope and to the King. His devotions were to all people in charity and his duty, to maintain the safety of the king's highway over the Mersey, was therefore a duty to all God's travellers.

The establishment proved to be a success and was described as a going concern in the time of King John (1199–1216). That the Priory had official recognition is proven in that Gervaise of Canterbury includes the house in his list of religious houses at the end of the Mappa Mundi dated 1200.

When completed, the buildings comprised the church and bell tower, the nave of which opened at either end into the cloister measuring 66ft from north to south and the chapter house, which was entered from the cloister and is today still a practising chapel.

Constructed entirely of the original Norman fabric, the lower room of the chapter house was surrounded with stone seats for the monks. The upper room of the chapter house was added in the 14th century and is thought to have been used as a Scriptorium (a writing room, where manuscripts were made). Sadly no such work

The crypt interior at Birkenhead Priory.

on Birkenhead has been discovered. No records were made of those stirring times, or of the personalities who passed across the ferry or through the Priory gate.

From the chapter house a passage led to the Dorter, or sleeping quarters, of the monks on the first floor. A large infirmary for the sick and aged, especially those invalids who had been blooded, was adjacent to this section of the Priory and near to the kitchens. North of the cloister was the Frater – the brothers' dining hall. A guest hall of equal dimensions incorporating a vast fireplace adjoined the Frater.

There was, in addition, a large kitchen for preparation of food for guests and an accompanying Buttery. Adjacent to the Buttery was the Crypt, or sub-vault which

Birkenhead Priory crypt.

provided accommodation for ordinary guests. Superior guests were cared for in the large guest-hall to the west of the site. Above the guest-hall was the Prior's lodging, complete with separate entrance, stair and solar chamber. Mostly in ruins now, the Priory remains proof that the buildings were well organised, and fine examples of Norman architecture.

Nothing remains of the original church, which was completely rebuilt in the 13th century, and now only the ruined west wall of the rebuilt church remains. All told the Priory, at the height of its importance during the 15th and 16th centuries, must have been a beautiful establishment in an idyllic setting, well known and well used by local residents and

The crypt, west entrance.

Birkenhead Priory. The north range of the 14th-century quadripartite vaulting of the undercroft, below the refectory. It survives intact.

Birkenhead Priory, the buttery.

Birkenhead Priory showing the doorway from the cloister to the guest hall and (above) entrance to the Prior's chapel.

travellers alike – the sparkling jewel of Birkenhead. The pious industry of the Black Monks had accomplished much and it is stated in records of the time that beautiful buildings were erected and maintained without much cost.

The Priory never became a rich house. The original manor and lands were small and can never have been very productive. However, the location was important, especially to the kings of the period up to the 14th century – for the Priory stood on

Entrance to the Priory
chapter house chapel. St
Mary's spire is in the
background. On the right is
the stairway to the upper
room – possibly the
scriptorium or copying
room.

a major route to the North and West, and gave access to the rebellious military might of Wales and the Scots. Thus the king, who needed to ensure safe passage for his troops into Wales and the Northern territories, made use of the ferry. In the care of the church this became a secure and certain king's highway.

The monks provided succour for the poor local community, according to their rule, but inevitably disputes grew up between the clerics and the peasantry since both offered a ferrying service. While the monks gave their service as a devoted charity, the peasants made their living out of the service.

The Prior would draw on local people for labour on his estates. William (the gardener), Henry (the woodward) and John Becheton were all employed as servants of the Prior in 1376. Nicholas Barbour of Tranmere, a servant in 1508, stole the Prior's silver ring and was later convicted of the offence and hanged at Chester Castle. Relations remained uneasy. The ferry became heavily used and passengers would frequently look for shelter and lodging at the Priory. The Monks of the foundation were unable to cope with the cost of hospitality. The ferry passengers were a broad cross-section of mediaeval society: clerics, merchants, pilgrims, military men, princes and kings.

Having already obtained the protection of King John in 1201, and increasingly impoverished over the years, the Prior was obliged to seek help of the highest authority – the King himself.

The Priory proved a convenient meeting point when seeking allegiances in times of crisis and impending war. In 1275 Edward I came to the Priory during his

Birkenhead Priory chapter house built in the 14th century. The lower room was used as a chapel after the Dissolution in 1536. Photograph c.1896.

conquest of Wales. He failed at this time to draw Prince Llewellyn to Chester there to receive his homage. Nonetheless Edward's visit was a success and resulted in a request that the Prior provide a 15th of moveable goods for the King's projects of the time.

The poverty of the Priory became all too evident in 1277 when Edward returned and held an audience of five days, from 1 August, to receive envoys from the King of Scotland. Robert, son of Robert the Bruce, and the Bishops of St Andrews and Dunblane sought to settle disputes over boundaries of Church lands. This event is faithfully recorded and now commemorated in a stained glass window in Birkenhead Town Hall.

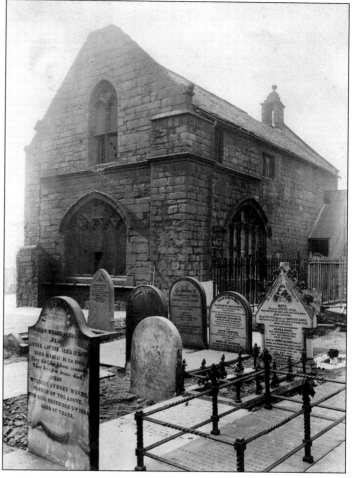

The same building from the Priory graveyard c.1896.

These visits were hugely expensive for the Priory. Apart from hospitality for Edward I and his court retinue, lodging and catering for travellers made great inroads into the Prior's treasury. The Prior petitioned the King and on 20 February was given permission to erect lodging houses and sell provisions for the care of the ferry users, many of whom were delayed for long periods during heavy weather which prevented them from crossing the Mersey.

Some remuneration was thereby gathered by the clergy. It was only by a Royal Charter of 1330, and after a second supplication, that Edward III granted the Prior sole rights of ferrying passengers, horses and other freight, and of charging ferry tolls. Civil disputes ceased between the monks and the peasantry.

And so the nobles stepped aside after 1400 to make way for men of Birkenhead. Those who toiled for the Prior and his disciples. Those who skirted the hard rule of the forester and his officers, for although the aforestation of Wirral restricted farming and cultivation within the main area of the peninsula, the Prior and his estates were royally excused the forester's strict regulations. There were attempts made to entrap the monks in devious rules of game and grazing. All accusations of infringement proved illicit and unwarranted. The Prior held his dignified place, punctilious in defending his manorial rights in the consistory courts at Chester, Willaston etc.

Thus accusations as to felling timber (124 oak trees in the Wirral Forest), slaying a buck stag in Claughton and creating a mill-pool or 'stagnum' within the Forest of Byrkehed, all of which actions would have limited the King's hunt for game, were countered by successive Priors between 1200 and 1376. The few convictions usually resulted in a minor fine, at most 13s 4d.

The Priory was also concerned in matters of everyday life and human interest

The Priory ruins – a column preserved c.1897.

The chapter House, altar and chapel in 1978.

outside clerical life. The records of the Wirral Hundred Courts and County Courts at this period show the Prior keenly involved in protecting his community. In 1309 Prior Robert stood surety for a fine of 40d levied against Matthew, son of Henry de Walley, who had killed a man in self-defence though had been mortally wounded himself.

When, in 1345, William, son of Hugh, was wounded with an arrow at Liverpool, he was taken across the river to the Priory. There he died and the verdict was murder, though no culprit was discovered.

The Prior served a complaint against Richard de Vernon, vicar of Bromborough and Dean of Wirral in March 1376–7. Richard had taken four pence by extortion at Bidston, from the Prior's servants William the gardener, Henry the woodward and John Becheton.

Prior Roger de Tiddesbury acted in charity and compassion when he pardoned William the Carter of Claughton in 1374. William had stolen some of the Priory cattle. Roger recovered them and took William back into his employ.

In 1409 brawling took place in the Prior's wood. William Nore from Lancashire lay in wait for draper Richard le Mosse of Liverpool and beat him. William was

Priory ruins, 1978.

outlawed from Cheshire for this and nine years elapsed before he paid his fine of 26s 8d.

The overwhelming calamity of this period was the Black Death. There were two visitations of the plague, the first in 1349, when the abbot of Chester was fatally infected, and another in 1369. In Liverpool across the Mersey in 1361 the strike of a deadly pestilence was growing daily more grievous. Although no records of plague deaths at Birkenhead exist, it is unlikely that this house escaped any more lightly than other monasteries which were reduced to a mere handful of men, both within their walls and on their estates.

Later in the 14th century there was an increasing movement to improve the lot of the peasant classes. In 1381 Wat Tyler led the agrarian rising against the harsh regime of ecclesiastical landlords. The movement was mainly in the eastern counties although there was one outbreak against the Abbot of Chester. The King's general proclamation against unlawful risings and meetings of the people was read at the County Court of Cheshire on 23 July 1381 and later on 27 July in the parish church of Eastham.

Serfs of the abbot were known to be meeting secretly in the woods and fields of Cheshire whilst funds were being privately collected. A large body of serfs rose under arms, terrifying the city and the county. The rising was immediately quelled. Men were arrested and thrown into gaol in Chester Castle and the funds were confiscated. The abbot of Chester and all the ecclesiastics of Cheshire suffered great unpopularity as a consequence. The monks of the Priory of Birkenhead would have

Priory graveyard, 1978.

suffered similar reactions from the local populace, with resultant hostility and bad will on the part of potential employees and tenants of the Priory estates.

The practice of selecting a Prior was by unanimous election on the part of the brethren of Birkenhead, after obtaining permission of the founder.

A satisfactory list of the Priors of Birkenhead cannot be compiled for the first 100 years due to lack of records. From the 14th century the list is probably complete and notably English. It begins with Robert, elected *c.*1190–1206 and ends with John Sharpe, a monk of Birkenhead, elected 1519 and who served until 1534 when the Dissolution ended his service.

According to records, three of the Priors appear to have had somewhat colourful associations with Birkenhead Priory over its long history. In the early 1400s Richard Norman, a lad of 14, was in service to a member of the order of Austin Friars. The boy proved wayward and his master sought to discipline him, wounding him severely in the process. In defending himself, Richard drew his own knife and accidentally stabbed his master in the neck. The wound proved fatal and the Friar died a day later. This was a sacrilegious crime from which the Pope could absolve Richard Norman and, accordingly, Richard journeyed to Rome in the garb of a pilgrim. Despite the Pope's absolution and the penance he duly paid, Richard was still covered in remorse and sought peace by renouncing the world and becoming a Benedictine Monk at Birkenhead Priory. He sought further dispensation from his sins and received the Pope's blessing in 1435, eventually achieving election as Prior of Birkenhead *c.*1440. He died in 1456.

Thomas Reynforth or Rainford was elected by his brothers in 1462. The election was confirmed by the bishop's vicar general on 30 April that year. His tombstone is the only surviving identifiable tombstone and is important in that it proves that the

Priors were buried in the chapter house. In 1818 Thomas Rainford's stone was raised. The slab was then inserted in the external wall of the chapter house. In 1896 it was again removed during reparation work and set with cement in a wooden framework within the building. In 1913, during renovations, it was again reset in the floor at the east end of the building. The inscription reads 'Here lieth Thomas Rayneford a former worthy Prior of this House, who died on 8 May in the year of our Lord 1473. May God be gracious to his soul!'. When the stone was first raised in 1818 three well-preserved skeletons were found. Who they belonged to, and what subsequently happened to them, is now a mystery.

Prior John Sharpe was elected on 21 July 1519 on the death of Hugh Hyne. The election was confirmed at the palace of Lichfield. He arranged installation of a stained-glass window on the north side of Bowdon's church in 1530, just six years before the Dissolution of the Monasteries and the closure of Birkenhead Priory.

The window bears the inscription 'Orate pro bono statu Johannis Sharpe prioris de Birkenhead qui istam fenestram fieri fecit anno domini MCCCCCXXX.'

Also in the roof of the church, on the north aisle, were the armorial bearings of the Priory, namely the arms of the founder, Masey of Dunham (quarterly, red and gold, in the first quarter a silver lion passant) and over them in pale what has been described as a silver crozier turned sinister. The crook or crozier is a symbol of the Prior's spiritual authority and also the pilgrims' staff of St James the Great.

The suppression of the monasteries commenced in 1534 when a general survey of religious houses was made and Henry VIII appropriated revenue from all religious houses, abbeys and priories by Act of 1534. The monasteries, convents, abbeys and priories were finally dissolved by a further Act of 1536. The general survey of 1534 resulted in charges of a gross and incredible nature being lodged at many of the religious houses.

St Mary's Church pictured in 1978. After closure and partial demolition the remaining church walls were converted into an open-air theatre. This picture shows the project in operation.

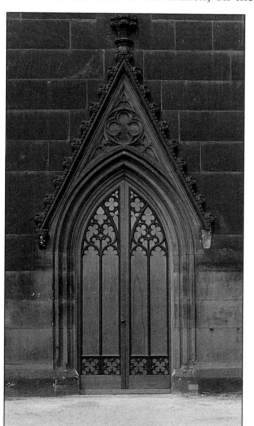

The restored doorway of St Mary's Church tower, 1919.

The report on Birkenhead Priory contains only one allegation – that a monk named Richard Chester was guilty of incontinence. Nothing was charged against Prior John Sharpe. The monks of Birkenhead made no resistance to expulsion, as there had been at Norton Priory. There the Abbot was hanged as a result of his treasonable rebellion. The Birkenhead monks left the Priory in May 1536, when the house was rendered to the King. Sharpe received an annual pension of £12, dating from 2 July 1536. The monks were allowed to choose to go abroad to religious houses or to be transferred to a reconstituted Benedictine foundation such as that of St Werburgh's Convent at Chester. Each monk was supplied with some clothing on his departure. It has also been stated, according to entries in municipal records, that some of the monks were later employed as bookbinders by the Mayor of Liverpool. No inventory of the contents and valuables of Birkenhead Priory exists. It is believed that all items would have been gathered into the coffers of the Augmentation Court.

So ended the holy era of Birkenhead. Few people knew that, beneath a column of the foundation stones, lay the skeleton of a wild sheep. A symbol of purity and peace, this token of the Lamb of God remained untouched and undiscovered until excavations of the ruins were carried out between 1913 and 1919. The bones were rescued and placed in a glazed case within the chapter house. They now form part of the historic exhibition relating to the Priory in the Crypt of the renovated ruins together with other artefacts. Also on display are a number of artefacts either surviving or uncovered during various excavations and renovations at the site. Among them: the heavy iron mediaeval keys of the main Priory gate; a gold noble from the reign of Edward III *c.*1361; a Nuremburg token used by pilgrims of the Middle Ages and entitling them to claim alms at religious houses; several sherds of 15th century roof tiles; a wild boar's tusk; and fragments of a green glazed pottery jug, probably made in the Saintogne region of France in the 14th century.

William Laird Esq, founder of Lairds, (1780–1841). He was buried in St Mary's Parish Churchyard on Priory ground. This painting is attributed to T.H. Illidge (1799–1851).

Thus Birkenhead Priory and Manor were rendered up to Henry VIII in May 1536, and Randle Arrowsmith was appointed Royal Bailiff with Randle Poole, of a Wirral family with a rather unsavoury reputation, as his Land Steward.

On 17 March 1544 Ralph Worsley of Worsley near Eccles, Lancashire described in *Letters and Papers of Henry VIII* as the King's servant, obtained a grant of all the lands and properties of the Priory and Manor of Birkenhead for a purchase price of £568 11s 6d.

Worsley was born around 1483. His monument in St Mary's Church, Chester states he had been a page of the wardrobe and steward of the chamber and, as such, was a vital member of the King's Household. He must have trailed the glamour of the 16th-century court life, for he was also King's Chamberlain; Crown Bearer; Keeper of the Royal lions, lionesses and leopards at the Tower of London; Grand Train

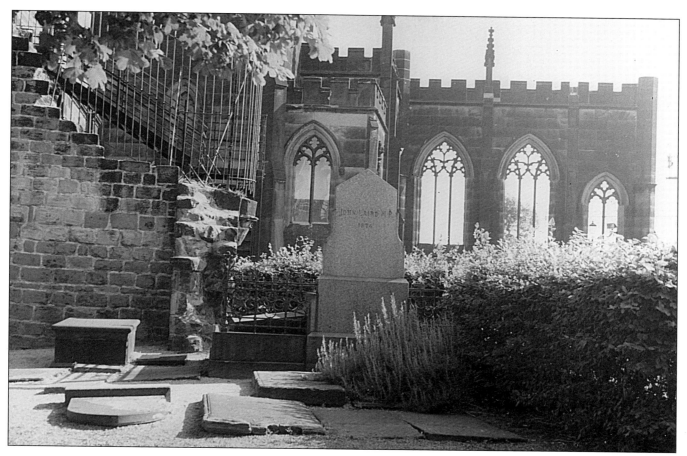

Bearer; Controller in the counties of Chester and Flint; and Escheator in Lancashire. He died in 1572 lauded for his superior mind, his piety and charity.

The Priory estates passed to his favourite daughter Alice and her husband Thomas Powell of Horsley Hall in Denbighshire. The Powells were more devoted to their Denbigh estates and allowed Birkenhead to sleep on until Sir Thomas Powell, a godson, Baronet and High Sheriff of Cheshire succeeded to the manor in 1628. During his ownership the English Civil War erupted. The Priory hostelry was garrisoned by Royalist troops in 1644 during the Siege of Chester. Defeating Charles I at Rowton Moor, the Parliamentary forces turned to quash all uprisings in Cheshire. The Priory was taken and dismantled. Doubtless the ordinary people of Birkenhead suffered badly during the turmoil.

Sir Thomas Powell died in 1694 without issue. His estates were sold to John Cleveland, who was Mayor of Liverpool in 1700 and MP for that city in 1710. The Clevelands built Birkenhead Hall in the grounds of the Priory, on land now occupied by Chester Street. The Priory ruins became a picturesque folly within their 18th-century gardens and many of the local residents were employed in their service. The ferry operated as always and was in control of the squire, though leased to local townspeople such as Thomas Barton who, in 1717, employed four ferrymen to sail three boats. Their wages were 5s per week.

Otherwise Birkenhead remained a tiny, rural hamlet, entirely overshadowed by the wealth and power of Liverpool. William Cleveland Junior succeeded his father and, on his death, the manor passed to his daughter Alice who had married Francis Price. The Price family held sway in Birkenhead from *c.*1700 until 1820 when their

John Laird's grave at Birkenhead Priory pictured in October 1991. Laird (successor to William) was born in Greenock on 14 June 1805, and died in Birkenhead on 29 October 1874. He was elected as the first MP for Birkenhead on 10 December 1855. His son John Laird Junior was the first Mayor of Birkenhead in 1877.

Woodside, Birkenhead seen across the Mersey from Liverpool in the 1960s. From left to right: St Mary's Church spire; Laird's yards; the ferry landing stage (foreground); the Woodside Hotel (background); the domed tower of Birkenhead Town Hall; and the Mersey Rail Tunnel tower at Hamilton Square Station.

lands were sold to the Commissioners of Birkenhead. The Prices were largely unremarkable as squires of Birkenhead with just a couple of exceptions. Richard Parry Price, was the son of Richard Parry Price FRS, a popular and well-respected landlord who died in 1782, and was buried in the Priory grounds where today a marble tablet in the chapter house records his goodly life. His son, also named Richard Parry Price, became squire in 1782. He assumed the name Pulestan and achieved a Peerage in 1813. He vacated the hall and built a property nearer the shore. Later Pulestan spent summers at Birkenhead living on a yacht moored in Wallasey Pool. The hall was sold to the Misses Kister who opened it as a boarding school for young ladies. Scandal erupted when one of the pupils eloped with a dashing major who carried her off to Gretna Green.

In 1801, at the time of the first organised national census, Birkenhead's population stood at just 110 residents. The township was by then a mix of mansions, farmsteads, inns, cottages and ferry-buildings.

Enter the second notable Price. In 1815, Francis Richard Price of Bry-y-Pys was the last squire of the manor. The age of steam had arrived on the Mersey and Price began to build properties on his land to draw new people to the town. He sought to attract Liverpool merchants to Birkenhead who could commute to Liverpool by way of his ferry services. In 1819 to enhance the area, and as an added incentive, he built St Mary's Parish Church beside the ancient Priory ruins.

His plan was a success and was partly responsible for drawing iron manufacturer William Laird to the natural port of Birkenhead. The result of Price's endeavour was that two imaginative minds were inspired with one idea, to develop Birkenhead as a grand new town and generate wealth for the local community.

Part 2
DEVELOPMENT AND GOVERNMENT-FUNDED PLAN
THE TOWN 1810 -1870

'LONDON is a modern Babylon; Paris has aped Imperial Rome;... disciples of progress... have great faith in the future of Birkenhead.' So wrote Benjamin Disraeli, Tory MP, and later Lord Beaconsfield, in 1847. Like a magical transformation scene, new Birkenhead in 1844 arose from the small village of earlier times, the brainchild of Francis Richard Price and then William Laird.

Both men realised that the new steam-driven sailing vessels could make the crossing to Liverpool safer and swifter than the Birkenhead ferry-boats. They knew that Birkenhead would prosper with improved and expanded communication with Liverpool, the rest of Britain and the world. Price, of course, owned the village and the ancient ferry-rights. Laird had purchased land from Price and established a boiler-works, and later a shipbuilding yard, on the shores of Birkenhead. All was in place for the development of a new and exciting town.

Laird's industrial works, established in 1824, stood at the foot of Livingstone Street. With Price's support he brought Edinburgh architect James Gillespie Graham to draw up a development plan for Birkenhead. Gillespie Graham was a self-made man of humble origins who achieved fame as an energetic and successful architect and married into the Scottish aristocracy. He designed many fine houses for the landed gentry and, in 1815, laid out part of the lower new town of Edinburgh. A fellow Scot of such importance and experience was the perfect choice for Laird's grand design. Graham's grid-iron plan of long, straight, wide avenues lined with stone-faced buildings of high architectural quality was hailed as fine, and ambitious.

Woodside Hotel at the top of the runway. A quiet hamlet as painted by W.G. Herdman in 1814.

Birkenhead Market 1845. A drawing by Charles Warren Clennell c.1846.

Money poured in from those seeking rich rewards, among them wealthy local men. Here came Sir John Tobin of Liscard Hall, Wallasey (formerly property of the Prior of Birkenhead and purchased from Price in 1838). Much of Tobin's wealth came from his involvement in plantations, and slave trade in the West Indies. His merchant wealth led to his election as Mayor of Liverpool in 1819. He was later knighted, and later again involved in the purchase of Wallasey Pool with the consequent Building of Birkenhead Docks. Tobin died in 1851.

Thomas Brassey was to follow him in seeking interests in the building of

Two views of Birkenhead Market 1845, from the Illustrated London News.

Birkenhead. At 16 Brassey was articled to a land surveyor named Lawton, land agent to Francis Price. Brassey succeeded Lawton in that role upon the latter's death. Ultimately he became a railway contractor, with operations throughout the world, and associating with stalwarts such as George Stephenson. It seems almost inevitable that his early business connections with Price, and with Birkenhead, together with his marriage into the Harrison shipping family involved him with the ambitious development of the town.

Sir William Jackson was equally significant in the development of Birkenhead. He formed an association with William Laird in his early 30s, having already retired from his wealthy merchant business in Liverpool and turning his attention to land-purchase in Birkenhead. In 1838 he was elected Commissioner of the town and, with Laird, became instrumental in building the city of the future. He purchased the Woodside Ferry and gave it to the township in 1841. He fostered the building of the Birkenhead to Chester Railway in 1840 and gave land for the foundation of Birkenhead Park. He again fostered the public park's creation to magnificent completion in 1847.

He seemingly supported all ambitious schemes, not least the building of the Birkenhead Docks and the gas and water works in 1842. His interest in the town was equally matched by William Laird, and their families were to become closer still when Jessie Laird married Geoffrey Jackson on 1 March 1893. With Laird and Francis Price at their head, these were the leading stalwarts who formulated the progress of Birkenhead in the 19th century.

As was evident in the selection of James Gillespie Graham, the best modern

Birkenhead Market as it looked in 1916.

designers and professionals were sought to build new Birkenhead. Joseph Paxton was chosen to design Jackson's Eden of a park. Paxton, from minor office as foreman of the Duke of Devonshire's arboretum at Chatsworth House in 1824, was promoted to superintendent of the gardens at Chatsworth in 1826. He was approached by Sir William Jackson in 1844.

Paxton's Birkenhead plans transformed the water-meadows, which had been Priory grazing land, into a recreation ground in two sections – north and south – with a wide carriage driveway dividing them. Peripheral carriage ways formed boundaries, and a classical triumphal arch was built at the main entrance, reminiscent of l'Arc de Triomphe in Paris. A further four gateways with palatial entrance lodges were built, each reflecting a different style of architecture: Gothic, Ionic, Italian and Norman. The garden was a triumphant blend of water features, palm-houses, bandstands, oriental bridges and the finest exotic plantings of rare flowers, shrubs and trees.

Since its grand opening in 1847, Birkenhead Park has been hailed as a model of finest garden planning throughout the world and is distinguished as the first park in this country to be provided by public subscription.

The Birkenhead Dock System was intended to be the life-force of the town, providing revenue, wealth and employment for the community. James Meadows Rendel, protégé of Thomas Telford and civil engineer of great reputation, was elected to draw up plans for the extensive project, which comprised Birkenhead's natural harbour and the waters of Wallasey Pool. Rendel's plans and building

St Mary's Church tower of 1829, within the grounds of the oldest building in Merseyside, Birkenhead Priory, which dates from 1150.

Claughton Manor House. The home of Sir William Jackson, dating from 1843–6 and designed by Charles Reed (later Charles Verelst). It stood on ground above Park Road East and was a veritable palace. It was described by Sir Nikolaus Pevsner in 1971, after studying plans, documents and descriptions, as 'A Graeco-Italian villa of exceptional quality and refinement'. It was demolished in the late 1930s.

Artisans' courts designed for working-class Birkonians by James Gillespie Graham in the 1840s. This is the back of Chester Street, near the shipyards and docks. The area fell into disrepair and neglect after the depression of the 1870s in Birkenhead. Demolished c.1920s and replaced with small red-bricked terraced properties.

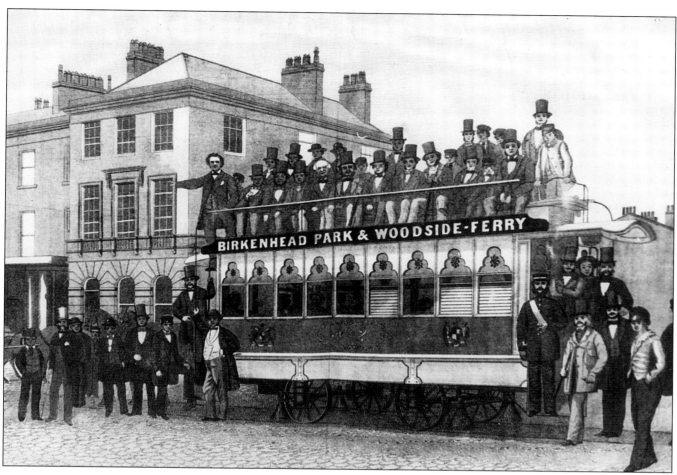

scheme were hailed as great, modern and far-sighted. Sadly the scheme eventually proved incompetent. Both Rendel and Birkenhead were ruined when, in 1858, rights to dock ownership and revenues were transferred to the Mersey Docks and Harbour Board in Liverpool. Those were dark days for Birkenhead, however, from 1839 to1847, Birkenhead seemingly had a golden future.

The first fine combined Town Hall and Market Hall were designed in Greek style and built by the architect R.B. Rampling in 1833. The market was of special importance being at that time the centre of local trade in the town serving farmers and trades people of Wirral districts. It was therefore akin to the centre of local government, a source of revenue, a source of good community spirit and communications.

In 1833 the Woodside Royal Mail Ferry Hotel opened. Today it survives – a relic of Birkenhead's existence as a resort and important mail-coach station serving London and the North of England. In 1833 the government had passed an Act to appoint Commissioners for the Improvement of Birkenhead. Development began in earnest and the plans begun by James Gillespie Graham in 1825 were carried forward to culminate in the noble and fine residential houses in Hamilton Square, where space was left for a magnificent centrepiece, the Birkenhead Town Hall. Many remarked on the similarity of Graham's designs in Birkenhead to those he had designed in Edinburgh.

Gillespie Graham's grid-iron plan for Birkenhead was based on a rectangle of long, wide, seemingly endless streets stretching from the West to the East where they

Birkenhead Street Railway. The first in the world opened 20 August 1860. George Francis Train stands, bareheaded, at the top of the stairs pointing towards Birkenhead Park. An American, Train was also a somewhat eccentric promoter, merchant and author who, during his colourful life (1829–1904), announced himself a candidate for the US presidency, got caught up in revolutions, was jailed for obscenity and travelled around the world in 80 days, inspiring Jules Verne. He also found time to introduce street railways to the world in Birkenhead in 1860!

Another scene from the same day. This time George Francis Train is standing on the driver's platform.

reached the grandeur of Hamilton Square, overlooking the river. The Classical square comprises four terraces of splendid houses, each in a slightly different architectural style, which surround a central garden. This was enclosed for the exclusive use of the residents with a roadway separating the houses from the garden.

Building began in 1825 and was completed in 1846. The exception to this was

The Great Float, Birkenhead Docks. The hydraulic tower and engine house of the Great Float was modelled on the Piazza Della Signoria of Florence (pictured inset). It provided power for opening dock gates and raising bridges. It was built to the design of John Bernard Hartley and was completed in 1863.

the Town Hall for which a site was reserved on the east side, though not filled until 1883. The buildings do not entirely conform to Gillespie Graham's high aesthetic standards. These proved to be too costly and were adapted, which largely accounts for the differing styles of the four sides of the square.

Originally planned as terraces of three storeys, the houses were to display pilastered doorways, wrought-iron balconies and were to have been faced with fine white Storeton stone from the local Bebington quarries.

The first houses were built on the east side, of which Number 63 was to be William Laird's private residence. His sunken garden is now a municipal car park and his house is converted to offices of the local authority.

It has been said that the dour dignity of these houses, and many in the town now demolished, was markedly Scottish in character and perhaps attributable to the personal influence of William Laird and his Greenock background. In 1877 a

statue of John Laird (son of William Laird) the first Member of Parliament for Birkenhead, was placed in prime position opposite the still-vacant Town Hall site. The sculptor was Albert Bruce-Joy, creator of many notable public statues – a statue of Queen Victoria which stands by the parliament building in British Columbia and a bust of poet Matthew Arnold in Westminster Abbey among them. The statue of Laird was relocated to the East side of the square in 1925 when Lionel Budden, a local architect and sculptor and H. Tyson Smith, himself a fine artist, collaborated in designing the Cenotaph which stands in its place today, honouring the dead of two world wars.

An Eleanor-style cross, in memory of Queen Victoria (1837–1901) by Edmund Kirby, local architect and resident of Birkenhead, was unveiled in 1905 and stands at the heart of the gardens which have been altered considerably over the years. The architectural historian Edward Hubbard regretted their 'facile formality bereft of large trees which would have offset the grandeur of the square'.

Between 1996 and 2003, the Hamilton Quarter has benefited from public funding to restore and invigorate pride in Hamilton Square and to establish a 'people's park' there. The intention was to provide a variety of street-entertainment and recreation on a pedestrianised plateau at the front of the Town Hall. The result was a square and Town Hall reinvested with a new dignity. Bereft of its role as centre of local authority since 1974, Birkenhead Town Hall now houses the Wirral Museum and Archives Service. The service specialises in the historic records and artefacts of Messrs Cammell Laird shipbuilders. The new Metropolitan Borough of

Marble sculpture of William Shakespeare, Reference Library landing, Birkenhead Library, June 1984. This bust was specially commissioned by the Birkenhead Literary and Scientific Society in 1864, on the 300th anniversary of Shakespeare's birth, and presented to the Free Library as a gift to the people of Birkenhead. Since 1864 the bust has been housed in each of the central library buildings together with a special collection of books relating to his life and works. The marble bust was transferred from Market Place South Library to the new Birkenhead Library in 1933 and is displayed today on the upper landing adjacent to the reference department.

Houses in Price Street. It was intended that the entire town should consist of stone-faced buildings of high architectural quality. A number of fine-looking, three-storey terraces (of inferior social status to the much larger Hamilton Square residences) were in fact built, apparently in the early 1840s, before the town's economic difficulties set in and architectural aspirations were abandoned. This row is now demolished.

Wirral, which includes the County Borough of Birkenhead, is controlled and administered from the larger Wallasey Town Hall.

Building on Birkenhead Town Hall was delayed until 1883 and completed in 1887. It is an example of English Baroque Classicism designed by C.O. Ellison and Son and stands two storeys high with a grand pillared portico with a flight of steps at both sides, designed for ceremonial occasions. Inside there is a grand staircase and lavish council chamber. Over the staircase a window designed by Gilbert P. Gamon 1904 commemorates the visit of Edward I to Birkenhead in 1277.

The building was damaged by fire in 1901 and restored by Henry Hartley who rebuilt the tower to a new design with a dome. The Town Hall still dominates the Square and both have been the setting for many grand occasions, as well as important local events.

On 23 October 1844, processions commenced there in celebration of the laying of the foundation stone of the new docks. Three years later, on Easter Day, 5 April 1847, fireworks and galas were staged as the docks, and the unique public park, were opened by Lord Morpeth, Queen Victoria's cousin, who gave his name to the dock. In 1850, on 27 November, Catholic riots broke out in Hamilton Square when magistrates convened a meeting in condemnation of the Pope's establishment of an English hierarchy and episcopacy and the rioters proceeded to the Town Hall. They attacked the premises and the 50-strong police-force was overwhelmed by thousands of mainly Irish labourers. The rioters then paraded, victorious, through the square. Several of the rebels were later arrested and imprisoned.

The arrival of George Francis Train of Boston in 1860 – a Yankee entrepreneur of colourful character – who presented credentials to the Commissioners of Birkenhead, resulted in the town providing the first street railway in Europe. Train grasped modern ideas with enthusiasm – he was a keen supporter of universal

suffrage in his motherland and, following an 80-day trip around the world, became the inspiration for Jules Verne's Phileas Fogg. Train was allowed to lay his line from Woodside Ferry to Birkenhead Park, bordering Hamilton Square. The railway was opened on 20 August 1860, for a trial period of six months. Train, who would later run for the US Presidency, and join the French Communist Party, believed in publicity and gave a great banquet to mark the opening. He

St Catherine's Hospital entrance, pictured August 1991. Built in 1862 as Tranmere Workhouse and administered by Birkenhead Guardians of the Poor until 1930 when it became Tranmere Infirmary.

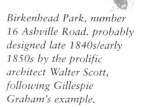

Birkenhead Park, number 16 Ashville Road. probably designed late 1840s/early 1850s by the prolific architect Walter Scott, following Gillespie Graham's example.

The first Birkenhead Post Office, built in Conway Street in 1856. Typical of the Classical style of Birkenhead buildings at the time. The upper floor became the second Birkenhead Library in May 1857. Appropriately accessible to the Telegraph Office and next to the funeral directors. Pictured in 1908.

Albert Memorial Industrial School, the archway over the entrance to the building. The school was built 1865–6, Sir William Jackson's gift to the town by local architect David Walker. The photograph was taken shortly before demolition in 1969.

invited all the European heads of state, including Queen Victoria, the Pope and Garibaldi. All were sadly, but perhaps unsuprisingly, otherwise engaged. Regardless, the proceedings were a great success and the railway carried 5,000 passengers on its first day of operation.

1860 marks the zenith of Birkenhead's glittering development. Plans were laid down, fine buildings were raised, gas and water systems were installed, great docks were planned and some constructed, a notable public park was established, road and rail communications were founded, and the creation of a light and airy town, for the enjoyment of all Birkenhead's people, began. Additionally there was a high level of employment, a healthy trade and new shopping areas like the Waterloo Buildings as well as appropriate accommodation for most residents, from the wealthy landed gentry, to the tradesmen and the artisan labourer. William Laird's dream had been to

Flaybrick Hill Cemetery,
Bidston, 1972. Building by
Lucy and Littler 1862–4,
layout and landscaping by
Edward Kemp, a pupil of
Sir Joseph Paxton and head
keeper at Birkenhead Park,
the laying out of which he
supervised for Paxton. A
pair of chapels separated by
a central spire in lively mid-
Victorian Gothic style.

St Mary's Church. Built
1819–21 by Thomas
Rickman, adjoining the
Priory ruins at the
expense of F.R. Price.
Part of his plan for
developing Birkenhead as
a resort.

create a town where all might live in healthy conditions according to their means. Laird's Birkenhead was truly a town to accommodate, amongst others, his own employees in the shipbuilding industry and all those who had been encouraged to enter Birkenhead to find work. A town with plentiful housing, new roads and modern facilities, Birkenhead thronged with families. They came from underprivileged parts of the country where work was scarce and the living hard. People came to Birkenhead from the surrounding parts of Lancashire, from Wales and from Scotland and many came from Ireland where the Potato Famine of the 1840s had left so many in desperate circumstances. The town nurtured a rich blend of cultures which has coloured its history to the present day.

Just like the town, William Laird's business thrived and expanded. His first graving-docks and shipyards were set up on the riverfront, between 1853 and 1856. His first steel ship was built in 1858. *The Illustrated London News* described it as '...the first instance in which steel plate has been used for this purpose'. The *Ma Robert* was a paddle steamer built by Laird for Dr David Livingstone's expedition on the Zambezi. Livingstone came to Birkenhead to supervise the loading of this small steamer on to the ship which was to take him to Africa. He stayed with John Laird, son of William, in his home at 63 Hamilton Square.

Monument to Sir William Jackson (1805–1876), in Flaybrick Cemetery.

The Woodside Hotel, built in 1833, was a survival of Birkenhead's existence as a resort. The once-symmetrical principal elevation has had recent alterations and additions. Photograph c.1971.

An 1870s view of Woodside.

The Laird Shipyards now became the mainstay of work and employment for the majority of people in Birkenhead from 1858 until closure in April 2001. A thriving port needed transport for cargo and passengers and a railway was built. The Birkenhead to Chester Railway opened in 1840, to a plan of George Stephenson. To mark the opening, 23 September 1840, a grand race was staged from Tranmere to Chester, between a coach and four, *Old Time*, and a train, *Young Steam*. The train won by miles, arriving early in Chester.

Hydraulic tower, Birkenhead docks. The upper stages of the tower have been removed since this photograph was taken in the 1890s. The lantern was lost in the bombing of World War Two.

The Birkenhead Terminus Station was in Grange Lane and the railway was amalgamated with Birkenhead, Lancashire and Cheshire Railway in 1847. That line was bought up by LNWR and the GWR companies in 1860. When the line became Birkenhead's direct link with London, a train, tram and ship terminus was opened at Woodside Station in 1878.

This period also saw the rapid expansion of the town. By 1861 Birkenhead's population had reached 35,929 and Parliamentary Borough status was granted. Birkenhead now included the neighbouring districts of Claughton, Oxton, Tranmere

Opened by theatrical entrepreneur Dennis Grennell in 1868, Argyle Theatre and Hotel became the best-loved British music hall when managed by Dennis J. Clarke from 1888 to 1934 and after his death by Tom Clarke, until bombed to ruins on 21 September 1940.

Victorian offices surrounding Hamilton Square, pictured October 1991.

A symmetrical block in Market Street. The window surrounds are typical of the town centre commercial buildings of the period. Cornice and rusticated ground floor.

and Rock Ferry. An election was held in December 1861 and John Laird stood as Conservative candidate against Thomas Brassey junior, the Liberal candidate. A legal challenge brought by Brassey concerning suitability of John Laird's supporters delayed the proceedings and was regarded as scandalous affair on the part of Brassey, who first lost favour with the electorate and subsequently his seat to John Laird, who became Birkenhead's first MP, a position he maintained until his death on 29 October 1874.

John Laird shone as a philanthropist, following his father's fine example. The Lairds were intent on serving their workforce and the people of Birkenhead. Good working and living conditions meant a contented workforce – and this was their aim.

John Laird carried these principles further. On 16 February 1856, he called the first public meeting of ratepayers to establish a public library service in the town. Self-education had arrived.

Birkenhead adopted the Public Libraries Act of 1850, just six years after it was passed. A library rate of 1d in the pound was levied – money set aside for purchase of books by Commissioners – and a Lending and Reference Library was opened on 3 December 1856, in premises in Price Street. No doubt Francis Price was smiling angelically upon the proceedings. Between 300 and 400 people were visiting the library daily. From this day onward there was a definite thirst for education in Birkenhead.

John Laird realised that the good health of the community was an essential requirement in the town. To that end he was to finance the building and management of the Birkenhead Borough Hospital which opened in 1863.

All seemed thriving but, from being a potentially wealthy town, Birkenhead was now about to face the threat of decline. The great opportunity for prosperity had been wrested from the people of Birkenhead in 1858, when the operations at Birkenhead Docks were transferred to the Mersey Docks and Harbour Board. A scandal had broken out when it was revealed that J.M. Rendel, architect of the dock scheme, had proved incompetent and the Trustees of the Dock were now bankrupt. 'The best part of a quarter of a million pounds had been squandered and wasted. The great dock enterprise which was to revolutionise the commercial world, was ruined!' (Sulley: *History of Ancient and Modern Birkenhead*) .Rendel's plans and work were found to be unsafe. He was obliged to resign. James Abernathy, formerly Surveying Officer to the Admiralty, replaced him. Modern Birkenhead still bears the scars of this blow to her economy and which arrested the further development of the town.

Houses in Lord Street. Quite humble two-storey terraces, but still stone-faced, classical and carefully proportioned and detailed. Now demolished.

Queen's Hotel, Park Road East, 1972. Italianate design, stucco, of three storeys and nine by four bays. Ground floor with ionic pilasters and porch. Apparently early 1860s.

Opening of Birkenhead Park, 5 April 1847. It was the first publicly-funded park in Britain.

Birkenhead Park main entrance as it looked in November 1991.

Birkenhead Park was laid out 1843–7 to the designs of Joseph Paxton. The Lower Lake boathouse stands part restored. The cast-iron bridge and this, the Swiss Bridge remain as here, admirably restored in the 1950s/60s.

Lower Park Lake, Birkenhead Park.

Palm House, Upper Park, Birkenhead Park.

Birkenhead Park.

View in Upper Park, Birkenhead Park.

The Rockery, Birkenhead Park.

Birkenhead Park Boat House. Originally intended as a bandstand, the pantile roof and earliest balustrading have now disappeared.

Central Library, Hamilton Street. The first purpose-built library in Birkenhead, opened in 1864.

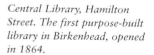

The 1868-built Argyle Theatre, Birkenhead, a 1920s view of the interior. Seen here are the auditorium pit, dress circle, boxes and gallery. The wheel in the top balcony was a projector for colour spotlights. Coloured triangles of celluloid were fitted into the wheel and used to change colours on the stage.

Part 3
EXPLOITATION
TO 1900

DESPITE the dip in her fortunes during the 1860s Birkenhead was firmly established as a Parliamentary Borough. Improved communications, both road and rail, the introduction of gas, water and sewerage services, and the use of public buildings brought the affairs of Birkenhead and its neighbours into close relationship.

Facilities for culture and entertainment had been introduced as early as 5 April 1847, when Hendry's Booth opened. Performances at Hendry's Booth were rapid-fire. Richard III would pursue his wicked career in 20 minutes flat. Plays were carefully designed to prevent flagging audience interest, and to consistently fill coffers. The town centre close to the market housed many theatres and circuses. Birkenhead Music Hall was built in Claughton Road and opened in 1862, at the same time as the foundation stone for Birkenhead's Borough Hospital was being laid by the Marquis of Westminster. The Workman's Hall, later Queen's Hall, also in Claughton Road was built in 1865. The Theatre Royal in Argyle Street was purpose-built and designed by Lewis Hornblower, an architect who had been involved in the design of Birkenhead Park. Regarded as a 'first-class temple of Thespis', the Royal opened in 1864. It was later bought by W.W. Kelly, local actor and town councillor. His wife, the beautiful actress Edith Cole, is still remembered for her performances as Empress Josephine in *The Royal Divorce* at the theatre. She played opposite her husband's Napoleon in which role he became famous for his line 'Not tonight Josephine!'. The Kellys sold the theatre in the 1920s and it was later converted into the Savoy cinema. Today it is an entertainment centre.

Providing lighter entertainment was Ohmy's Circus in Grange Road, opened in 1888 and later named Theatre Metropole. It closed in 1905 and later became Birkenhead C.W.S. Living which itself closed in 2000. The best known and most beloved of Birkenhead theatres was the Argyle Music Hall opened in 1868 on a site in Argyle Street. This theatre had something of a sleazy reputation at first. It was a typical Victorian Palace of Varieties, where theatre and public house bar were

closely associated. Performances on stage could be raw, and verged on the outrageous. Dennis Gramell the Irish publican and owner of the Liverpool Rotunda was to bring his nephew D.J. Clarke into the business in 1888. Clarke was intent on raising the tone of the Argyle and set about improving her fortunes, and reputation, from 1892 until 1940. Those Birkonians who enjoyed musical performances were

Hampton House, the first town dispensary, founded in 1828 on the corner of Oliver Street and Hampton Street. It was later used as a centre for the able-bodied unemployed by the Birkenhead Union.

Cental block and tower of St Catherine's Hospital, Church Road, Tranmere. originally the Birkenhead Union Workhouse, built 1862–3 and designed by Thomas Leyland. Photographed October 1977.

Now a farmhouse close to Bidston Church in School Lane, this 17th-century building was the Ring O' Bells hostelry, mentioned by Dickens and owned by Simon Croft ('Simon the Cellarer'), well known for his ham and egg menu. After his death in 1864 the pub acquired a rather more unsavoury reputation and was closed down in 1868.

well catered for from the 1840s to 1944 and through to the present day. Concerts of professional musicians were provided at Birkenhead Town Hall in 1842, under the patronage of Lady Cust of Leasowe Castle. Other venues were church based: Cathcart Street Baptist Church (1908), Clifton Road Congregational Church (1909), and the YMCA Hall in Grange Road all played host. Performances at the latter of Handel's *Messiah* by the Birkenhead Philharmonic Society thrilled full houses in 1911. The Craven Rooms provided annual concerts of the classics and soprano Anne Romer starred there on 22 September 1849.

As early as 29 April 1842 the Assembly Rooms of the Albion Hotel gave a 'Verbal and Instrumental Concert' which featured the soprano Miss Delcy of the Theatre Royal, Drury Lane. A charity performance of *The Gondoliers* was staged at Birkenhead Town Hall on 8 May 1893 in aid of the Borough Hospital. Claughton Road Music Hall, in 1898, provided a concert by the Gitana Ladies Choir, Winners of the National Eisteddfod Prize. The Birkenhead Male Voice Choir was formed in the 1940s and performed at the Concert Hall at Byrne Avenue Public Baths. Here was an echo of Easter Monday, 31 March, 1902, when Eisteddfod Gadeiriol of Birkenhead honoured the Welsh community. This Birkenhead 'Young Mens Eisteddfod' was held at Queens Hall, Claughton Road.

It is not surprising that theatre, music and the arts should be well received by the people of Birkenhead. The broad band of cultures and nationalities of the people lent them sensitivity and instinctive appreciation of the finer things of life. These qualities were also to cause them frustration when hard times resulted in loss of employment, poverty and sordid living conditions for so many following the fiasco of the Dock Scheme failure in the 1860s and 70s. Families which had migrated from great distances to what must have seemed like he 'silver city' in the 1830s and 40s, found themselves stranded in the north End of the town in properties which soon became a welter of insanitary neglect. Other properties like the artisans' dwellings, designed by Gillespie Graham in 1830, fell empty and deserted, becoming potential slum dwellings.

In the 1860s the Mersey Docks and Harbour Board continued the rebuilding of the Birkenhead Docks and the repair of all damage resulting from J.M. Randle's bad workmanship and design. The Great Float was completed in 1863. The work was slow and the Board was somewhat resentful because John Laird insisted that work should concentrate on the completion of the Alfred Dock and the Low Water Basin, whilst the Board was impatient to proceed with work in building Bootle Docks. This disagreement, and resultant delay, may well have resulted in lay-offs and shortfalls for the workers of Birkenhead, many of whom were, by coincidence, Roman Catholics.

In 1862 there was much sectarian tension in Birkenhead. Local Orange Lodges clashed bitterly with the Roman Catholic community. Both sects were supported by their sympathisers in Liverpool.

In Birkenhead Dr Joseph Baylee, an evangelical Irishman and Protestant vicar of Holy Trinity Church, was known for his zeal in attempting to convert Catholics to the Protestant religion. He had interests in Guiseppe Garibaldi's attempts to conquer the Papal States as part of unifying Italy as a republic. On 8 October 1862, Dr

Birkenhead Market Hall, Market Place South built 1843–5. The engineers were Fox, Henderson & Co, later to build the Crystal Palace for the Great Exhibition of 1851, to Joseph Paxton's design. This is an early morning in 1895.

Argyle Theatre in
the late 1940s,
only a shell after
the blitz of 1940.

Baylee held an open meeting, advertised with posters in bright orange, to discuss Garibaldi and the Italian situation. Given that much of the surrounding community were of the Catholic faith, Dr Baylee's very visible support for the cause only served to inflame an already simmering situation. A riot erupted and some 4,000 Irishmen converged on Holy Trinity Church vandalising property and attacking those who restrained them, including Police officers. They were only appeased when priests from St Werburgh's Church in Grange Lane called for peace, although describing Garibaldi as a viper and an enemy of the Pope.

Undeterred, Dr Baylee held his postponed meeting at Holy Trinity on 15 October 1862. The County Constabulary arrived to keep order in support of special constables from the Cheshire Volunteer Rifles and workmen from Laird's. At 7am thousands of Irish men and women, carrying staves and in belligerent mood, swept along Price Street to Holy Trinity Church. Despite an attempt at peacemaking by Father Goulding, the appearance of police at the scene prompted the Irish to attack. Fighting went on until 10pm. Fire broke out in cottages belonging to some of the Irish community all around Holy Trinity; almost every man in the Birkenhead Police Force received injury; and many of the Irish resorted to stoning opponents and adjacent property. Inspector Burgess and PC Morris died in the rioting.

When the trouble ended, eleven men had been arrested and taken to the Bridewell. On 16 October, 12 Irish people were brought before magistrates at Chester Castle. The prisoners were remanded, awaiting trial, by Sir Edward Cust. They later received sentences ranging from nine years to six months. The national newspapers condemned the Cheshire magistrates for losing control of the situation and there was evident fear in the press that such civil rioting might be contagious.

After this affair the tensions between Orangemen Protestants and Irish Catholics were never eased. The differences were to affect personal relationships, friendships, employment, local community matters, management and organisation, housing, segregation and division of the classes. Though it might at first have appeared to have been the case, the riots had nothing to do with Garibaldi. This was a 'war' between the privileged and the underprivileged, that pitted working people without work against authority. It was a sectarian conflict between supporters of the Orange Order and Roman Catholics. Down

Woodside Station of 1878. The original booking hall, in the form of a mediaeval great hall, with open timber roof, pictured November 1967 near the end of its days.

the years there would be repercussions, no heroes and two martyrs.

Noticeable hardship for much of the community was becoming evident. Hungry, ragged, barefoot children begged for coppers on the streets. It was a practice that was to continue until the end of World War Two. The North End of the town became the domain of the poorest people and the area of worst neglect. From Flaybrick Hill at the outskirts of the town and a block of purpose-built dockers' flats named Queen's Buildings (better known as the Dock Cottages), small properties bordered the docks and dock railway into the industrial zone of small factories, workshops and shipyards at the back of Hamilton Square. These were properties specially designed for the labouring classes who entered Birkenhead in the 1830s. The same families who were unemployed and impoverished. Queen's Buildings were five tall blocks of tenements with flat roofs for hanging out washing. All apartments had gas and running water and the ground floor had

Another view of the booking hall in Robert Edward Johnson's Woodside Station. It featured decorative brickwork and iron work of complementary design. This fine main line terminus building was demolished in 1968.

shops as well as a licensed pub known by the somewhat colourful name of the Blood Tub. This complex, designed by C.E. Lang, was quite revolutionary and modern. It had its own church, also by Lang, dedicated to St James. The pub provided earthly sustenance, the church sustenance of the spiritual kind. At least, that was the intention, but there was little likelihood of sustenance without the means of livelihood.

The Chester Railway of 1840, and the extension along the docks, was to drive a wedge through Gillespie Graham's elegant gridiron street plan. A jigsaw puzzle of land parcels resulted, many of which were unsuitable for purposes other than rubbish-tips or scrapyards and so became unsaleable, much as they remain today, perpetuating an unpleasant aspect presented by the town even today.

This was a perfect set-up for the carpetbaggers who established somewhat sleazy businesses of questionable purpose from the 1860s and 70s onwards, and who exploited the poor as a cheap labour market. Due to the changed image of the town and the spoil of industry, including the profitable Laird's shipyards, the wealthier town residents, who had occupied better housing in Hamilton Square and adjacent fine properties, began to move away to cleaner, healthier suburbs. They took residence in Oxton, Claughton, Prenton and Noctorum. Though Sir William Jackson had built his grand hall and estate, Claughton Manor in 1846, well in advance of the 60s and 70s.

But what of the abandoned detritus of the community? Who cared for them? As it turned out, there were many who cared for the suffering. Laird, Brassey and Jackson were three in particular who, having reaped large benefits from the development of Birkenhead, had sufficient conscience to return some of their gains to those in need.

Brassey had become an important international railway contractor when, in 1852, he won the contract to build the Grand Trunk Railway of Canada. He opened a works in Birkenhead, opposite the Great Float, to construct the vast amount of railway equipment he needed for 540 miles of railway. The engineering works, which he named Canada Works, opened in 1853 and employed 600 people. They were paid an average of £1 a week and it was well noted that all of Brassey's navvies ate 2lb of beef per day. Indirectly Brassey sought to help and educate the population, albeit concentrating on his own workforce. He provided a library and reading room with a stock of some 600 books.

Up to 1866 the Canada Works made and supplied railway equipment and components for many engineering projects and railways around the globe in countries as diverse as Austria and India. Building bridges over the Jumna River and the construction of a vital 40-mile supply route from Balaclava to the front line during the Crimean War were just two examples. In 1866 there was a slump in railway construction and Brassey lost trade. He died in 1870 and, after a rapid decline in business, the Canada Works closed in 1889, leaving more people unemployed and poor.

Sir William Jackson had been involved in all the ambitious projects to create the new Birkenhead. Some of these came about only because of his imaginative foresight; several, such as the park, of lasting importance. Jackson had also worked with Thomas Brassey on important contracts – the most notable of these being the Grand Trunk Railway of Canada. In 1864 Jackson donated land for the building of the Birkenhead industrial school. The school was to stand in the centre of the poorest area of Birkenhead – on Corporation Road in the heart of Dockland. In addition to being a memorial to the late Prince Consort, the school was to provide

The covered platforms at Woodside Station.

education and care for 120 boys and 60 girls from poor homes in the locality. The Albert Memorial School opened in 1865 entirely at Jackson's expense. One of the prime aims of England's industrial schools was to provide a decent education outside of the workhouse and of correctional establishments and many boys were sent there by the magistrates. It is said that, by 1870, some 423 children had been rescued by the school from degradation and a life of crime. They were given shelter and food and trained for work as sailors, navvies in the mines, electricians and farm labourers. Sadly, conditions were considered less than ideal and the industrial schools proved somewhat controversial. At Birkenhead there were deaths among the boys, seldom explained. Other boys absconded or proved unsuitable and were returned to friends or to the workhouse. And though some did benefit from the scheme, 423 children was merely a very small drop in a very large ocean.

William Laird's ambition in developing Birkenhead and establishing his shipbuilding business, was to create a sound living and working environment for his workforce. His son John followed his example. Their schemes in the town were designed to cater for all levels of society and the Lairds organised their shipyards to provide comfortable and efficient working conditions for the men.

The slump of 1860 had affected the Lairds as it affected the rest of the townspeople. A depression set in. John Laird provided assistance by way of his institutions: the hospital; the public library; the School of Art; and in his support of all major developments including those concerning the supply of gas and water and the improvement of the transportation system. After he became the town's first MP

Birkenhead Park football club 1880–1. Back row (left to right): W.P. Evans, G. Cowie, C. Phillips, G. Stewart, B.B. Middleton, R. Wood, H. Brandon, J.H. Black, J.R. Wilson. Middle row: Archie Williamson, John Ravenscroft, H.M. Blythe, D.A. Bingham. Front Row: A.C. Blain, G.K. Smith, J.B. Barry, E.A. Beazley.

Ohmy's Circus Theatre, Grange Road, built 1888,
later the Gaiety. Later again W.W. Kelly's Metropole
later, in 1913 the Hippodrome and later again(!) the
Birkenhead Co-Operative department store.

he continued to represent Birkenhead's interests at a national level and promoted the interests of the Cheshire Volunteers. Birkenhead was incorporated on 13 August 1877 and John Laird Junior was elected first mayor on 20 November 1877. His public mayoral service continued together with his brother William until the late 1880s.

The Poor Law Amendment Act of 1834 encouraged the Guardians of the Birkenhead Union, a body of wealthy and upstanding men, to establish a workhouse at Tranmere in 1861. Despite their best efforts it seems, with hindsight, unlikely that those raised in luxury could entirely understand the lot, or the needs, of the impoverished 400 people who were housed in this 'Palace of the Poor'. The original building was of meagre provision and Board minutes of the period show a dismal picture of the inmates' harsh life. Whilst they had a roof over their head, and basic food provision, the men, women and children of the workhouse were expected to labour hard for their charity – in part a side-effect of an intention to make the workhouse a last resort.

In 1862–63 there were 1,223 deaths of which 470 were children under two years. In that year also 2,377 babies were born, many to unmarried mothers. There were many instances of what were described as 'lunatics' being removed from the workhouse. Those seeking assistance due to straitened circumstances were assessed at the Guardian Offices in Hampton House, Oliver Street. The stigma of disgrace and fear associated with workhouse attendance was to survive several generations and to outlive the days of the workhouse itself.

In 1930 the role of the Guardians was taken over by the Public Assistance Committee. The 1930s proved to be a similar era of economic slump and depression. Tranmere Workhouse no longer took inmates, its premises had been much improved and its role was by then changed to that of a hospital with good

Birkenhead Park entrance, from an old postcard c.1890.

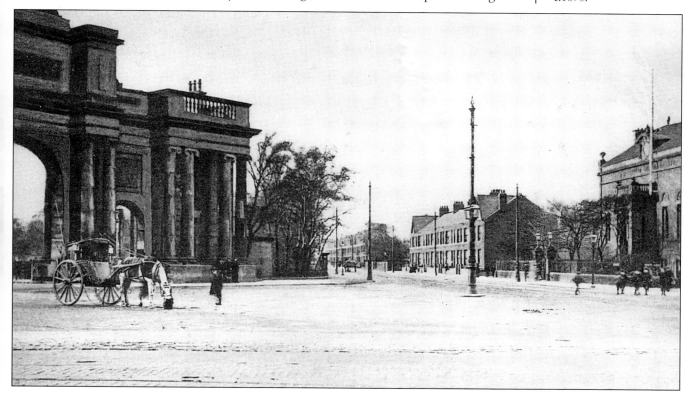

Birkenhead Borough Hospital c.1890s, from a postcard. Built in 1862–3 at the expense of John Laird, it later became Birkenhead General Hospital.

medical and nursing services. Under the P.A.C. Birkenhead Corporation now tried to look after the poor in a more individual way. The old workhouse is now renamed St Catherine's Hospital and is part of Wirral's health services.

Charles Thompson, the 'Poor Children's Friend' (1841–1903), founded Birkenhead Poor Children's Mission in Hemingford Street in 1892. Thompson's object was to alleviate the sad condition of those children who, through the neglect of parents or the pinch of poverty, were reduced to extreme destitution. Charles Thompson stated that he was drawn to Birkenhead by God in the 1860s. He began as a grocer in Price Street and attended Oxton Congregational Church. He spent the whole of his life caring for destitute children and their families at the North End of Birkenhead, and all others who needed his help. He persuaded the more fortunate members of the community, including William Hesketh Lever, to finance a distribution programme of free food, clothing and recreation for the very poor. On Christmas mornings, and on many other days, queues of 2,000 or more children might be waiting at the doors of Thompson's Mission in Hemingford Street. He and his family toured the borough bringing children to the mission, visiting sad families, providing practical care and peace to the down and out. He died on 13 February 1903 and was mourned throughout the town. Even Queen Alexandra sent her sympathies to his family.

Thompson's work continues to this day. His wife, and then his daughter Annie, continued to run the mission and established a trust fund to finance its work. Annie Thompson died in 1965 and Mrs Jones and Mrs Lowry took over the mission until it was absorbed into the Liverpool City Mission in 1987. The Revd Rob Jeffs has served as its minister and organiser since that date.

The mission's doors are open to people in need from all walks of life: those with addictions, lone-parents and their children, elderly pensioners, the young, the sick,

the homeless and the heavy-hearted. Charles Thompson's work continues unabated.

In 1881 the population of the new borough was 84,006 with Oxton, Tranmere and Rock Ferry now within the borough boundary. A township on the suburbs of Birkenhead, Oxton had become a fine residential area from its origins as a small village in the ownership of the Earl of Shrewsbury. Tranmere had very ancient importance as a manor and its people remained very independent even after incorporation. Its acquisition became vital to the development and expansion of the Laird shipyards, the ferry-boat services and the increasing population. Eventually Birkenhead absorbed the area and built houses and its workhouse there. Royal Rock Ferry, next down the coast to Tranmere, had been a small township important mainly for its ferry company, and for its potential as a Mersey riverside residential neighbourhood for wealthy Liverpool merchants.

Laird's continued to thrive, providing plenty of work for the population. In 1862 a ship known only as 'Hull 290' was launched. Weighing some 900 tons, she was fitted out as a cruiser and had gun emplacements but no guns. Her eventual destination was officially unknown and when left Birkenhead she bore the name *Enrica*. In August that year, off the coast of the Azores, she was officially commissioned as the *CSS Alabama* – a vital and notorious piece of the Confederate Army's battle plan during the American Civil War, carrying a crew of 120 men and 24 officers. During her 22-month career at sea she cruised the oceans from the eastern seaboard of the US to the South China Sea – her aim to disrupt her enemy's

Some members of the combined Birkenhead police and fire force, c.1880.

trade routes. Her crew boarded some 447 vessels, captured 65 Union merchant ships and sank the *USS Hatteras*. In compensation for her actions, the British government was required to pay the United States £2million – a considerably greater fee than that received by Laird's for her construction.

Larger ships of more than 3,000 tons were being constructed at Laird's, mostly merchantmen like the *Queen* in 1865, and the *Spain* in 1871 for routes to New York. Sailing ships gave way to twin-screw engined vessels of 10,000 tons and battleships of 14,000 tons, ships like *HMS Glory* and *HMS Exmouth*. Orders came in from British Government, and from the governments of Chile and Argentina. Though Laird's were successful, the town continued to become ever more shabby and numbers of poor grew continually.

It was in 1863 that a group of influential men led by John Laird Senior, and including several notable clergy, including Canon Andrew Knox, met in the Music Hall, Claughton Road and formed Birkenhead Provident Benevolent Society. They drew up a plan for alleviating the problems of the poor and underprivileged people of Birkenhead. Poverty was an overwhelming and increasing anguish in the town. Begging and vagrancy were abiding problems and were considered entirely unacceptable. Women whose husbands had left town on 'tramp', deserted their families or gone abroad; or old and infirm people permanently incapacitated were not entitled to relief. For them, the only option was the workhouse or worse. The Board of the Birkenhead Provident Benevolent Society were to provide relief to all persons in temporary distress. The sick, the unemployed, widows and the ailing elderly on Parish Relief all qualified for Society help. The Society also encouraged the poor to save by depositing money with the Society and was an early example of a credit union.

Birkenhead Children's Hospital, built in 1882–3 by John Clarke.

Woodside Ferry pay booths, c.1890s.

To our modern sensibilities the Birkenhead of those days seems desperate and stricken. In the intervening years, spurred on by witnessing those conditions, the BPB Society tried to meet the needs of the community and blossomed into what would become the Birkenhead Council of Social Service, which eventually fostered the Unemployed Activity Centre, Citizens Advice Bureau, Youth Advisory Council, Association for the Disabled, Old Peoples Welfare Association, Adult Reading Project for illiterates, and Relief in Sickness Charity. By 1900 the Society had moved its headquarters from 115 Market Street to 46 Hamilton Square. The demands for help had increased and would continue to do so.

Many positive changes took place in Birkenhead from 1870–1900, despite the reduced circumstances of many townsfolk. The creation of the town borough and John Laird Junior's election as mayor in 1877 were followed by Alfred Gill's appointment as first town clerk in 1880 and as Clerk of the Peace in 1882. Birkenhead was truly gaining its own distinct identity. The Arms of the County Borough, drawn up in August 1878 were described thus:

Town Coat of Arms.

'Birkenhead (Cheshire) Quarterly Or and Argent on a Cross Gules between a Lion passant of the last in the first quarter, an Oak tree issuant from a Mount proper in the second, and Etoile Azure in the third, and two Lions passant of the third in the fourth, a Crosier in pale of the first, and two Crescents in fesse of the second. The Crest: On a wreath of the colours Upon a Rock proper in front of a Crosier erect, or a Lion Azure resting the dexter paw on an Anchor also or.'

The principal heraldic devices were taken from the seals of the several local governing bodies of the townships which were brought together to form the Borough of Birkenhead.

Roberts & Co, tea merchants, Ferry Approach, Woodside, c.1900.

HMS Mars, a first class battleship, 14,900 tons, 12,000 hp and top speed of 18 knots. Pictured in 1897, she was built at Laird's and launched in the previous March.

The Pastoral Staff and the Lion formed part of the seal of the Extra-Parochial Chapelry or Township of Birkenhead. The oak tree was the main feature of the Tranmere Local Board, the star is representative of Bebington and the two lions in the fourth quartering of Oxton. The crosier on the perpendicular bar of the broad cross originally formed part of the Prior's arms.

The motto 'Ubi Fides ibi Lux et Robur' means 'where there is faith, there is light and strength' and was suggested by Canon Tarver of Chester, who stated that he had 'sought to bring out the two ideas, the religious sentiment and the union of the four townships... taking the Cross and Pastoral Staff as suggesting 'Faith', the Star and Crescent [representing] 'Light' and the Oak and Lions [representing] 'Strength'

As was the case in so many British towns in the 19th century, one of the key components in the establishment of Birkenhead as a thriving community, if not economy, was the extension of the Chester railway to Woodside Ferry in 1878. Robert Edward Johnston's Woodside Station was built in 1878. Architectural historian Nikolaus Pevsner regarded it as one of the few really good mainline termini outside London. Sadly this gem of Victorian architecture was demolished in 1968.

In 1886, after many harrowing disasters and fatal accidents among the workforce, the Mersey Railway Tunnel was opened. The lines of communication between Birkenhead and Liverpool were now opened wide. The tunnel had to be graded steeply (to 1 in 30 on the Liverpool side) due to a problem in the river bed. Water seepage, at the rate of 9,000 gallons per minute, also caused alarm. Today this figure stands at only 4,000 gallons a minute. The use of the Beaumont rock boring machine enabled rapid progress during tunnelling of an inch per minute). However, use of the Beaumont resulted in the whole crew of seven operators dying from silicosis a few years later. Despite the setbacks and tragedies, the railway was opened by the Prince of Wales (later Edward VII) on 21 January 1886 and the first passenger trains passed through the tunnel on 1 February 1886. It was not until 1903 that the Mersey Railway was electrified. The tunnel service proved a detriment to Birkenhead traders and shopkeepers, since the townsfolk were travelling to

Manor House, Higher Tranmere. A 17th-century building, demolished in 1906.

Birkenhead Town Hall, Hamilton Square. A wartime (1940–5) view showing the rebuilt tower following the 1901 fire.

Liverpool for finer shops and goods. Others were finding travel to the city easy and so in looking for employment across the river they were creating a vacuum in the workforce. The tunnel, supported as a project by Gladstone, proven feasible by the engineers Brunlees and Fox, was the forerunner of the much desired road tunnel across the Mersey.

In 1885 the 21-acre Mersey Park was opened in Tranmere and in 1881 Birkenhead Corporation had acquired the 45-acres of lawns and hills that made up Thurstaston Common beside the Dee. These were the first exercises in providing recreation areas for the townspeople, a necessity to combat the somewhat unhealthy environment in a crowded town of Birkenhead's size. Victoria Park of 29 acres was later opened in Tranmere in 1901.

The health of the townspeople became a primary concern of the borough in the late 19th century. In 1883, to much celebration, the town's Children's Hospital on Woodchurch Road, was opened by the Duke of Westminster. It replaced several successive smaller hospitals which were inadequate to the needs of a town in which so many children lived. Many juvenile deaths were attributable to the insanitary dwellings and courts of the 'slum' neighbourhoods. The new hospital was further extended in 1903, with a large new outpatients department in addition.

In 1887 a great event was celebrated with appropriate pomp and ceremony. The grand, long-awaited Birkenhead Town Hall was opened in Hamilton Square. The building, by C. O. Ellison in restrainedly classical style, matches that of Bolton

Grange Road, 1910. From the left, at 181–183 Charles Foster, seller of fruit, fish, game and poultry; at 187 W.H. Harker & Co shoes; and at 191–193 Arthur Austin, clothier or seaman's outfitters.

Town Hall, although a central clock tower shows more imaginative treatment than that at Bolton. In 1901 a fire damaged the tower, which was rebuilt and restored by Henry Bartle. The opening ceremony was performed by John Laird, the borough's first mayor. The staircase window was replaced with new stained glass, representing Edward I's visit to Birkenhead Priory in 1277 and designed by Gilbert P. Gammon. The building is of Storeton Stone from the ancient local quarries and so particularly apt.

Annie Thompson, superintendent at the Charles Thompson Mission for poor children. During World War One she entertained wounded soldiers both at private Sunday gatherings and at the mission, which was open to all men needing assistance. Charles Thompson outings for the wounded were famous throughout Birkenhead. Annie carried on the charitable children's work of her father Charles Thompson after his death, aged 61 on 13 February 1903. Miss Thompson was awarded the MBE in 1953.

Birkenhead, which had been so quick to adopt the Public Libraries Act of 1850 and opened a library for the enlightenment of the townspeople in 1856, was slow to provide public education. The Education Act was passed in 1870, but the Birkenhead School Board was appointed as late as 1893. Birkenhead had chosen to provide 'voluntary, denominational education', housed in church premises. Church of England Schools were extended. A School Board was rejected in 1871 and again in 1875. The Church and Catholics of the town had opposed the proposals. In May 1882, at the instigation of the Revd William Binns, HM Education Department issued a final notice requiring the erection of new schools in Birkenhead and Tranmere within six months, failing which the Department would cause a School Board to be formed for the district. In haste, the School Attendance Committee built St Luke's School, Tranmere; Mersey Road School, Rock Ferry; and Borough Road Schools in the centre of the town.

It is something of a paradox that the first chairman of Birkenhead School Board in 1893 was Revd Andrew Knox of St Anne's Church, Beckwith Street. Although he had championed church schools, and managed those of St Anne's and at the Borough Hospital, he had vehemently opposed the appointment of a School Board. His church was at the hub of the poorest areas of Birkenhead. He established a day nursery, a flourishing Sunday School, a Samaritan Fund, Bands of Hope, Mothers' Meetings, Clothing Clubs, a reading room for young men and a parochial library. He was a Freemason and his charity was unstinting. He believed that board schools would exceed their functions when they became antagonistic to the voluntary system.

Public schools in Birkenhead have been a great credit to the town, providing many eminent members of society, of local and national importance. Birkenhead School opened in 1860. Many of the town's dignitaries held office as governors, William Jackson, John Laud, the Bishop of Chester, Professor James Bryce of Oxford among them. The school had an extraordinary record of success with numerous illustrious pupils. F. E.Smith, who became Lord Birkenhead, H. Graham White, president of Liberal Party in 1954, 'Sandy' Irvine and George Mallory, Everest mountaineers, and Andreas Whittam-Smith, the journalist who founded *The Independent* in 1986 and became a film censor, are five of the best-known old boys.

In 1883, the Birkenhead Institute was founded by George Atkin of Egerton Park, Rock Ferry, and others including Tom Oakshott of Rock Ferry, owner of Messrs G. H. Lee – a leading department store of Liverpool – and Thomas Deakin of Birkenhead

The course of instruction was to fit pupils for commercial life, civil service, university and industry. Due to the depression of trade in Birkenhead, the school opened only in 1889 with 42 pupils. The success of the school grew and in 1908 it was taken over by Birkenhead Board of Education. Many local personalities were educated there. The most famous was the World War One poet Wilfred T. Owen MC, a lieutenant in the 2nd Manchester Regiment who was killed at the front on 4 November 1918. Sir Henry Cohen, a pupil from the age of 12 in 1912, was Professor of Medicine at Liverpool University and one of the greatest physicians of 20th century.

1883 saw the foundation of the High Schools Company for Girls Ltd, in Oxton, Birkenhead. The governors, like those of the Boys' Schools, wished to establish a good academic education for girls in an area more convenient to Birkenhead than the city of Liverpool. The Birkenhead High School building was a palatial mansion called Belgrano. Since that time, the school has provided some of the best education for girls in the country and prepared some of the best brains for famous careers. Actress Patricia Routlege (born 1929), and financier Nicola Horlick (born 1960) are but two of the girls who were educated here. These schools were the first notable schools to provide good secondary education in the borough.

Now, at the beginning of a new century, two significant new services were introduced. In 1896, an electricity generating station was opened in Bentinck Street. The days of gaslight and fuel were numbered for, although the townspeople were apprehensive of the new service, the advantages of clean fuel and instant, brilliant light were recognised, and soon two generating stations were to supply 1,730 consumers. The future was set for an electric light show as public events of the town would bear witness.

Water shortages were a problem for the people as early as 1890. Three pumping stations did not provide the town's water supply. Water had to be rationed by hours of the day, according to district. Plans had to be made to build a dam to supply Birkenhead. The Alwen River in Denbighshire was chosen to provide the Alwen Gravitation Scheme which was to open in 1921 and slake the thirst of Birkenhead.

Thirst first, health and hygiene next. With water at a premium there was little to encourage personal hygiene. Many homes did not have facilities for bathing and washing, until the opening of the public baths at Livingstone Street in 1900. This provided a private baths suite and laundry at nominal charges, for the use of all individuals. This was luxury for the ordinary man, woman and child of the town. If one was to eradicate disease, it was necessary to provide a means of cleansing as well as medication. The recreational provision of two swimming pools was also available and, according to the town's minutes, well-used. The local police force had

Morpeth Docks and pumping station c.1920. The first stage of the Birkenhead Dock Scheme was opened Easter Monday 5 April 1847 by Viscount Morpeth, the same day that Birkenhead Park was opened.

special arrangements for their use of the pools. These baths were closest to working-class flats and tenements. At this time, expenditure for suitable washhouses throughout the town was not proportionately large.

The health of the town was parlous, especially for the poorer people in the squalid cottages and tenements in the dock areas of the town. In 1863, some 195 people died of smallpox. In 1877, 608 cases of smallpox were treated, from which 93 people died. It was believed that the disease had been brought to the town by foreign sailors on the dockyard slips in Wallasey Pool. Dr Francis Vacher, the Medical Officer of Health, managed to contain the contagion until the danger had passed, although his junior house surgeon, revered in the town for his untiring devotion to the victims, died of the disease. He was only 23 years of age.

A fever hospital was opened in the centre of town to cater for the sick on visiting shipping. The risk of smallpox was eventually eradicated by a vaccination programme. But infant mortality was too high and due largely to the squalid living conditions of the poor families in the dockland areas, courts and cottages. The need for public health services and public hygiene became ever more apparent as the century drew to a close. The wealth and success of the leading citizens was a marked contrast to the sad state of the poor working people of the town.

Part 4

LIGHT AND DARK, WEALTH AND POVERTY. EDWARDIAN PERIOD TO 1914. SOUNDS AND ALARMS

THE 20th century began with the promise of a glittering future for Birkenhead unfulfilled. Queen Victoria had died on 22 January 901. Her son, the pleasure-loving Prince of Wales, was now King Edward VII.

The Queen was commemorated with a Queen Eleanor Cross confection at the heart of Hamilton Square Gardens. These gardens would be acquired by the Corporation of Birkenhead for the pleasure of the townspeople in 1903. King Edward's role in the opening of the Mersey Railway Tunnel and Mersey Railway, when Prince of Wales, would also be preserved after his death. The Clock Tower at Central Station and Clifton Crescent commemorates that event. Both of the memorials are, appropriately, by Edmund Kirby.

This was also a time of war – the Boer War. The volunteer regiments of Birkenhead had been formed following a call from John Laird Senior in 1859. There were eight companies. The Birkenhead Company drilled at 100 Church Street and in a field adjoining Bridge Street (shades of the Roman centurions!).

In 1882, the companies were renamed the 1st Volunteer Battalion, the Cheshire Regiment, or more commonly the Cheshire Greys, from the colour of their uniform. 1899 saw the outbreak of the Boer War. The Cheshire Greys were on active service in South Africa and on their return were given a civic welcome. Originally displayed in Grange Road West Drill Hall, a plaque dated 5 November, 1902 records their courage. It is now in Birkenhead Town Hall. In all, 149 soldiers of the regiment served in the Boer War. Four men of the regiment fell in battle. Captain Gordon

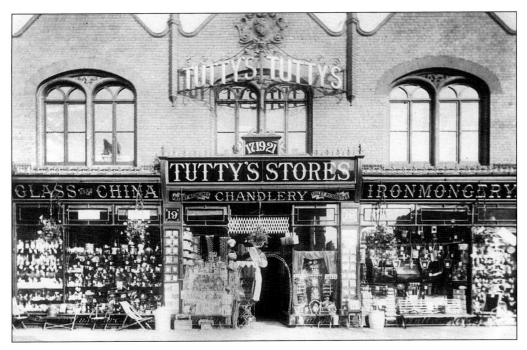

Laird was also one of the war dead and his mother, Mrs John Laird, gave a donation to the new Birkenhead Company's Drill Hall in her son's memory.

On 15 November 1902, Lieutenant-Colonel F. W. Blood, commanding officer, paid tribute to those who served in South Africa. He said, ' ... should occasion again arise ... .the battalion would emulate the spirited and patriotic response that was made to the call for volunteers in the hour of need and national danger'. His words were soon to be realised. Lieutenant-Colonel Blood, well loved by his men, was respected in the town. He retired in December 1906.

The population of the town, in the census of 1901, had increased to 110,915. The need for better public services and better communications was ever more urgent.

Rising population required more housing. Estates spread over almost all land north and south of Birkenhead Park; over all of Tranmere Hill, as far as Bebington Road, up the slopes to Prenton and Oxton and over the lowlands along the river front to Rock Ferry. For each house built there was a family that needed food and other commodities. Shops and shopping patterns began to change. Gillespie Graham's fine purpose-built shopping centres on Market Street, Conway Street and in Waterloo Buildings, were now too fine to cater for the ordinary working-class husband and wife. The main shopping centre moved to the centre of town, on Grange Road, Charing Cross, Exmouth Street and Oxton Road. Shops and hostelries became the required institutions.

The Birkenhead Market, that athenian temple of trade on Market Place South, continued to be the hub of commerce and activity in the town. The place where all would gather to gossip and find a bargain, much as it is today, although relocated. Where country trader, farmer and catch-penny would set up a stall. Where every rogue in town, every beggar (of which there were many) would seek a quick penny. Shopping on Grange Road, Hamilton Street, Market Street, Borough Road, Exmouth Street and Oxton Road was, at this time, a colourful experience.

The variety of shops and emporia was broad, offering goods of every variety, the cheap-jack, the small industrial commodities, the fine and high-class goods. Here was Robb's Brothers' Department Store, founded in 1872, selling to the gentry kid-gloves, evening-gowns, watered silk, engraved silver, cut crystal and best household goods. Here was a palace decked in fine wood panelling, plush with a graceful staircase. The shop provided a restaurant where one might take tea whilst buying the best.

Birkenhead and District Co-operative Society Ltd was established in 1891 and had a membership of 315 by 1892. This store and its offices would provide bread, milk, coal, household goods, clothing, shoes and later banking. Reasonable costs and good value, with a system of dividends, it was ideal for the ordinary person in the town who had an eye for thrift.

Allanson's Department Store Ltd, Grange Road, had grown out of a small draper's shop owned by John Allanson and his sister, in Grange Lane in 1861.

The Allansons believed in supplying demand and prospered accordingly. The store was modern by the standards of 1900, when it moved to a large building in Grange Road. Its distinguishing feature was a system of automatic cash-machines which flew on cables back and forth across the ceiling, carrying pounds, shillings and pence from counter to central cash office and making a tremendous clatter.

Tutty's Stores sold glass, china, chandlery and ironware from large premises at the top of Oxton Road, on the edge of Birkenhead's busy shopping district. Business thrived and the owner, Fred Tutty, became a town councillor. By then Grange Road (formerly Grange Lane and earlier the monk's route from their grange to Woodside) had become a mass of shops. Liptons the grocers stood cheek-by-jowl with Robb's; Birkenhead Corporation's gas stoves shop stood next to an oyster sellers; Michael McCann's confectionery business; M. Saronie, photographer; Hubbard and Martin Ltd, bakers; William Pyke and Sons, watchmakers; James Mitty Ltd, tripe dresser; the Singer Sewing Machine Co Ltd, blacksmith Edward Goldsmith; Albert Harrison, lodging house keeper all

Mason vase. Presented to E.G. Mason, Mayor of Birkenhead in 1898 by the Della Robbia Pottery to commemorate the visit of HRH Princess Louise to the pottery in that year. Cassandia Annie Walker designed and decorated the vase.

Queen Victoria memorial, Hamilton Square, Birkenhead.

Della Robbia Pottery 1898. At left the Mason Vase in the making. Harold Rathbone is in formal coat and spectacles, seated centre. John Bowers is on the right with Cassandia Annie Walker immediately behind Rathbone. Company premises were at 48 Hamilton Square. Pieces of the famous ware can raise from £200 to £450 today.

opened businesses there. In addition, there was Bentley Brothers' pawnbrokers – just one of some 300 shops of this type in central Birkenhead alone.

This sample of business in Grange Road early in the century is typical of trading in the town – there were many other shopping areas all with a similar mix. They were found in Oxton, Claughton and Prenton and were essential to cater for an quickly increasing population.

Several hotels catered for visitors to Birkenhead. The two best known being the Grange Hotel at Charing Cross and the Woodside Hotel of long-standing good reputation since its days as a coaching-house in the early 19th century. Of hostelries, there were many and no doubt countless beer-houses and shebeens that were unofficial, where the poorer people were wont to drown their sorrows, at the docklands and north end of town.

The previous century's concerns about the lack of good sanitation and public health in general had not been resolved in the early part of the 20th century. The Medical Officer of Health and his Public Health Inspectors were expected to carry out inspections to prevent offensive privies, smoke nuisance, stagnant drains, cellar occupations by vagrants etc., insanitary shops and bakehouses. Working-class houses were of particular concern and inspection of these properties during 1899–1907 by the medical officer of health's public health inspectors gave plenty of evidence of unsavoury practices and much cause for concern. Many people were sick and dying thanks to their squalid living environment. In 1907 one child out of every five new born would die. It was recognised that the poor suffered from want of skilled medical

attention and nursing. Children in particular were neglected as regards sufficient food and adequate clothing in their early years. They became permanently weakened and crippled '...unfit to meet the strains of life which afterwards fall upon them...' Common causes of death included measles, scarlatina (scarlet fever), erysipelas (a severe skin infection), diphtheria, typhoid fever, diarrhoea, phthisis (pulmonary tuberculosis), cirrhosis of the liver, whooping cough and general atrophy.

At last the public health inspectors began to insist on changes and recommendations were met quickly. Cobble-paving, prone to collect pools of filth which were impossible to remove, was to be replaced by large paving-stones as soon as possible. House-to-house inspections were carried out. Gulleys and passage drains were periodically cleansed. Public fountains were scoured. Ashpit refuse was systematically removed. Common lodging houses were regularly inspected both day

The opening ceremony of the electric tramways, 14 August 1901 at Birkenhead Town Hall.

Corporation stables, Laird Street, c.1902.

OXTON AND CLAUGHTON CIRCLE VIA BOROUGH RD

BIRKENHEAD CORPORATION TRAMWAYS

One of a batch of 15 cars (Nos 45–59) built in 1901 by G.F. Milnes with American 'McGuire' bogies. This photograph shows the car as new with an open top. Top covers were fitted during 1904.

Mersey Underground Railway. The first electrified run was 1 May 1903.

and night. Overcrowding in cellar occupation was suppressed and compulsory lime-washing of workshops and premises like bakehouses, was introduced. Open sewers were closed down. Adulterated foods were confiscated. Of these milk, butter, meat and fish were most commonly found tampered with. Smallpox had been largely eradicated by 1907, due to the careful vaccination of all newborn children.

Inspection of properties in Egerton Street, Connor's Court, Albion Street, Taylor's Buildings, Alwen Street, Orderly Avenue and Orderly Place, gave rise to the Birkenhead Improvement Scheme of 1901. Rebuilding, renovation and improved sanitary arrangements were the first exercise in raising the town's standards in housing for the working-class and unemployed population.

It was only in 1915, despite the Birkenhead medical officer of health's repeated pleas for qualified maternity assistance for all mothers and expectant mothers, that a maternity and child welfare centre was opened. One year later the first Birkenhead day nursery was opened at 3 Cole Street, with a qualified matron and staff. Children of one month to five years, whose mothers went out to work were cared for from 7.30am to 7pm, at a charge of 4d a day per child or 1s 8d per week. At the same time Birkenhead Rescue Association for Mothers and Babies was opened in Palm Grove, to help unmarried mothers. Significant social reforms had begun to take place and would continue albeit gradually.

Other aspects of daily life were changing, too. The tram service had been electrified in 1901 and what had been a highly-popular service since its introduction as a horse-drawn service in 1860 was now even more attractive. The trams, which were built in Birkenhead by the Starbuck Car and Wagon Co and later by Milnes Voss & Co, crossed the town from Birkenhead Park to Hamilton Square and from Hamilton Square to New Ferry, outside the town.

The Milnes Voss factory workshop stood at 227 Cleveland Street for many years and was once the centre for a business that supplied tramcars to towns and cities throughout the UK and across the world. The early trams were of two decks. The upper deck was open to all weathers and usually occupied by the hardy male passengers, whilst the ladies were cosseted below, where they sat on plush seating, and benefited from venetian blinds which protected their delicate complexions. Ultimately open-topped trams proved impractical in busy towns. As well as the unpredictable and unreliable weather, the atmosphere of the town was dirty. Business was halted at peak periods, when all passengers would prefer travelling on the covered deck.

Milnes and Voss were losing customers until they diversified by producing top-covered cars. The first, in 1903 was provided for Sheffield Corporation. Birkenhead followed suit, with its electric tram-cars. At this point the Cleveland Street works was closed and the business moved to Hadley and sold to a German firm. The workforce was resentful since many were left unemployed. G.F. Milnes opposed the move but, as he was the smallest shareholder, had no say in the matter. In 1906, Milnes Voss re-entered the electric tram building business and operated, once more, from Birkenhead. This time they built tramcars for use in cities as far widespread as Durban, Darwen, Dundee, Caracas and Madras and their new, covered, electric tramcars were a roaring success.

By 1900 Birkenhead's inadequate police force, which had been overwhelmed by rioters in 1862, had been increased from 54 constables to 191, and now had its first chief constable. A separate fire service had been established in premises at Whetstone Lane. The chief fire officer was enlisted to supervise high fire-risk areas of the town, liaise with industrialists and architects and pay special attention to places of public entertainment.

The latter was of particular importance since, despite the hard and harrowing times which were affecting the town, this was a period of razzle-dazzle. Music hall reached a peak of popularity at the Argyle Theatre, due in large part to the imagination and enterprise of Dennis J. Clarke. Clarke was a shrewd business man, with a keen eye for talent. He let it be known that he would employ all and every aspiring variety artist on the Argyle Theatre's bill. The audience was the gauge of

Miss Edith Cole (her professional name) was the wife of W.W. Kelly JP, CC, of Birkenhead. Kelly owned the Theatre Royal in Argyle Street from 1898 to 1905 and Miss Cole starred in many of his plays. Her most famous role was Empress Josephine to Kelly's Napoleon in The Royal Divorce. *Edith was statuesque, auburn-haired and fair-complexioned. She was also a charity worker and was decorated by the King of the Belgians for her work with Belgian refugees in Birkenhead during World War One. Cole Street is named after her.*

Birkenhead General Post Office from a postcard sent in 1927.

Trams waiting at Woodside Ferry.

their success and in Birkenhead audiences were not slow to register either approval or disapproval. Many an international star was 'born' at the Argyle and many a variety career plummeted after a howling disaster on stage there. Clarke arranged special contracts for all his performers. As unknowns he engaged them for first performances at a very low fee and made them sign agreements to return to the Argyle at the same fee whenever required, regardless of their future success. Artists flocked to his theatre and to Clarke's instinct for potential success, so that the cream

of the variety theatre was ever at his beck and call and at very reasonable rates of pay. The Argyle became a nationally-known training ground for variety performers.

Clarke was both popular and well respected. His ambition had been to acquire standing, both for his business and his reputation and with that aim he entered local politics, eventually achieving alderman status. Clarke bought an estate in Higher Bebington and his family lived there until the mid-1960s. The Argyle boasted an international reputation and many of the finest entertainers began their careers there.

Harry Lauder begged Clarke to give him a chance at stage comedy on 13 June 1896. He sang and joked for an audience of Birkenhead and Liverpool-based

Briardale Road, Birkenhead, seen on a postcard sent in 1926.

Charing Cross, Grange Road junction, c.1905 with the Grange Hotel of 1840.

labourers and navvies, largely Scouse and Irish, avoiding his usual Scottish material for fear of bringing their wrath upon him. They cheered him to the roof demanding more. D.J. Clarke sent him back on stage to use his Scottish jokes. Quivering in front of the audience, he gave them everything and they brought the house down. That was the start of a success that was to culminate in knighthood.

Clarke also engaged George Formby Senior in the early 1900s, and launched him on a successful comedy career. His son, George Formby Junior the comedian, actor and ukulele player, had one of his first engagements at the Argyle in 1921. His performance was a total disaster and he was booed off the stage. Ultimately, though, this setback proved temporary and Formby enjoyed a long and successful career in which he earned 30 shillings per week in the early days, and went on to become a millionaire by his death, age 56, in 1961.

The ladies of the Edwardian vaudeville were regulars at the Argyle. Statuesque, befeathered and bejewelled Florrie Forde the noted 'queen of the singalong', and Kate Carney appeared there as did male impersonator Hetty King and Gertie Gitana who was soon to become a forces sweetheart and, later, Arthur Lucan's Old Mother Riley and daughter Kitty O'Shea.

But as the 1900s proceeded, new inventions and changes in fashion brought lulls in D.J. Clarke's business. The gramophone, the wireless and the cinema were exciting innovations that would measurably poach the theatre-going public. But Clarke was enterprising and was later to integrate the new media into his theatrical presentations.

York Place at the junction of Balls Road and Oxton Road. This was later 'Hawkins famous high class furnisher'. Sadly the building collapsed in 2003.

For this time, however, all was glitter, greasepaint and loud, bawdy, brassy music. Edwardians to a T for theatre. For those with more classical interests W.W. Kelly, actor and theatre-manager, ran the Theatre Royal which stood opposite in Argyle Street. Here the lover of drama was beguiled with plays like the musical comedy *Peggy Machree*, the spooky melodrama *Creeping Shadows* and *In Darkest London*.

Other areas of recreation were becoming available to the average Birkenhead resident too. In the interest of both public health and recreation Victoria Park was opened in Tranmere on 1 August 1901. The lawns and flowers which covered 29 acres and surrounded an old mansion called the Towers, became a popular haunt for all those seeking fresh air and exercise. Between the wars Tranmere Cross was erected there. This former village cross, carved in 1500 and broken and scattered through the district, was retrieved and remodelled in 1937 and replaced on the grounds at the entrance of Victoria Park.

The Young Men's Christian Association of Birkenhead had grown (in 1873) during hard times to help young working men of the town and keep them occupied in what free time they had and so out of trouble. From small beginnings in shop premises in Conway Street, the club was removed to purpose-built premises in Grange Road on 29 November 1890. The President, C.J. Proctor, had provided a comfortable home-from-home for young men, bearing a large portion of the cost himself. The rest was provided by local charity.

The association provided facilities for healthy exercise and physical development and, in line with the Latin phrase *mens sana in corpore sano* – 'a healthy mind in a healthy body', also provided relief from loneliness and an introduction to Christianity. The first YMCA Building in Birkenhead had been the original Post Office in Conway Street in 1874. The GPO building has the style,

The Conway School, Conway Street. 1905–6 by T.W. Cubbon. Art Nouveau with terracotta dressings and ornament.

Memorial clock opposite Central Station, Argyle Street, unveiled in October 1912 to commemorate Edward VII, who died in 1910. The King had opened the Mersey Railway's Hamilton Square Station on 21 January 1886, when still Prince of Wales.

85

Photographs of the Back Chester Street area 1900–10, later demolished as part of a slum clearance programme.

mahogany furnishing and evocative smell of the grand Edwardian offices and is today as it was in 1907. This new, grand, purpose-built General Post Office, designed by Walter Pott, was opened in Argyle Street in 1907.

One year later, on 24 January 1908, the Birkenhead YMCA was visited by Lieutenant-General Robert Baden-Powell, defender of Mafeking, gave a lecture in the Grange Road YMCA. The subject was, of course, Scouting. He cited good citizenship as the motivation of his Scouting organisation and appealed for men to carry out the same work in Birkenhead. Thus the Boy Scout movement came into being in the town, where it went from strength to strength – a real boon to the poor boys of the town. A tablet recording Baden-Powell's visit was installed in the YMCA building in 1910 and unveiled by the newly-knighted Sir Robert Baden-Powell himself.

Elsewhere in Birkenhead the increasingly unstable international situation, which had so far little affected everyday life, was paying dividends for Laird's. Since 1893 the shipbuilders had been constructing for the Royal Navy, building an array of warships, battleships, torpedo boats and destroyers. Among them the predator-like destroyers *HMS Thrasher* and *HMS*

Virago and *HMS Panther* and *HMS Wolf* and the battleships *HMS Audacious* and *HMS Exmouth*. In 1903 Laird's amalgamated with the Sheffield steel firm of Charles Cammell & Co Ltd. Times were changing and the newly-formed Cammell Laird would play an important role in the times ahead.

In the meantime there was to be a shift in the status quo in Britain. At midnight on 6 May 1910 Edward VII died. The people of Birkenhead expressed loyal sorrow at the death of their king and loyal congratulation at the accession of the new monarch, George V. Three days later Mr A.H. Arkle, Mayor of Birkenhead read the formal proclamation of George V's Accession. Even though the time was 5.15pm,

Arrowe Hall, Arrowe Park. Now Arrowe Hall Hospital, used as an annex to St Catherine's.

Shore Road pumping station, Woodside, depicting a late Edwardian street scene c.1910.

A typical family from the Chester Street area before being demolished in 1910.

On board the steam ferry, c.1910.

The 2nd Volunteer Battalion Cheshire Regiment. Formed in October 1914, they undertook air-raid duties, manned anti-aircraft gun emplacements and all matters of home defence. A total of 200 men enlisted for service abroad.

the ceremony was witnessed by a large crowd. On Friday 20 May, in memory of Edward, there was a national day of mourning. In Birkenhead a civic service and procession was held in St Mary's Parish Church. Services were held in all the town's churches. All businesses closed for the day and, across Birkenhead, black and purple drapes appeared – the colours of mourning and royalty. Royalism, and nationalism, was at its peak.

On Wednesday 25 March 1914, Birkenhead received a visit by George V and Queen Mary. Their majesties appeared on the balcony of Birkenhead Town Hall to the rapturous cheers of the Birkonian crowds. A visit to Cammell Laird's shipyards

was made, where both Queen and King showed avid interest. Before leaving the town the royal couple were invited to visit Bidston Hill. Bidston Manor and Hill, 200ft above sea level, were part of an ancient parish outside Birkenhead which had been a hunting ground and lodge for Lord Derby in the 17th century was later purchased by Lord Vyner, Crown Jeweller. In 1894 the corporation had acquired the common, the hill, the old lighthouses and cottages for the townspeople's recreation ground. The King was asked to open and extension of the park, King George's Way a grassy avenue from Upton Road.

Whilst the Royal Family was almost universally loved, there was widespread dissatisfaction brewing at the social and political discrepancies between different sections of society. In Birkenhead there was a loud cry in favour of votes for women who were, along with more than half of the male population (those who did not own property or pay rent of at least £10 per year, servants with no home of their own, criminals and lunatics) denied a voice in the British political system.

A report in the *Birkenhead News* of Monday 11 July 1910 regarding Mr F.E. Smith, the Birkenhead-born Conservative MP for Walton, stated, 'People are saying that a Birkenhead man will go down to posterity as one of the chief opponents for extending justice to women…'. In the Commons Mr Smith, a brilliant orator, had acidly opposed Mr Shackleton's Women's Suffrage Bill. At 38 years, Smith was already in the public eye and destined for fame, an influential political career and a peerage. Only three days earlier there had been suffrage demonstrations at the gates of Birkenhead Park. Mr J.H. Zeigler led the proceedings, supported by Mrs Zeigler, Miss New and Miss J.H. Willmer, scions of Birkenhead society. Miss Willmer, of the famous printing family, would later become editor of the *Birkenhead News* and take on the management of the newspaper.

The women's suffrage movement was looked on with sympathy in Birkenhead.

Albert Memorial school band c.1916. The band cheered the troops with dock and railside serenades, and performed at all charity events in the town during World War One. Mr J. Williams (school band conductor) is to the right of the big bass drum. Mr T. Patterson (superintendent) is to the left.

Many men supported the movement. Mrs Evans, Mrs Raffles Bulley and Mr Arthur R. Allerton all spoke in enthusiastic favour of the petition on this occasion. But there were plenty of opponents and it has been suggested that Queen Mary herself was among them.

Portrait of Councillor D.J. Clarke, JP, owner of the Argyle Theatre and Birkenhead Hippodrome.

It is significant then that Beatrice Webb should visit the town on Monday 18 July 1910. A noted political radical and activist she was also an important influence in the foundation of the London School of Economics. Mrs Webb attended the annual congress of the Royal Institute of Public Health and presented a paper on 'Prevention of Destitution' which would prove so apt for Birkenhead. Mrs Webb said 'We should never be able to pull down the death rate ...we should always fail to maintain any decent level of public health so long as we allowed destitution to exist amongst us.' She also had strong views on the need to help the poor improve their own situation rather than try to solve the problem with charitable donations. 'Poor Law Administration... must be swept away.' Mrs Webb believed that prevention was preferred to cure, 'to prevent chronic destitution which breeds dull despair and indescribable demoralisation to which so many thousands are condemned'. It's significant that Mrs Webb gave her address by way of her representative. She did not attend the lavish receptions and garden parties which were given by the Mayor of Birkenhead to honour the rich and famous who attended the congress of which Sir William H. Lever was the president.

Like so many towns, luxury and squalor existed side by side in Birkenhead. It was clear that social reform would come. Already members of what would become the Labour Party was effecting some change. They had arrived in Birkenhead championing the workers and supporting the trades unions, although they had lost Mersey ward by just 59 votes. Already strikes had taken place and women of the laundry workers had won a small victory over their employers and obtained improved wages. However, the dock board employees strike for improved pay met with an obstinate and autocratic response from the employers who refused to deal with unions.

There was still a shortage of hospitals in the town and 1913 saw the opening of Tranmere Infirmary, St Catherine's Hospital, and a further 596 beds for the sick.

It would be some time before political or social reform could be addressed, regardless of the amount of support it was gaining in Britain. The situation in Europe was becoming increasingly unstable and, whilst Britain officially appeared to pay little heed to matters outside her own borders, larger and more powerful warships, like the heavily-armed dreadnoughts, were being built.

Town Hall. After the 1901 fire the upper stages of the tower were rebuilt to a revised design by Henry Hartley. This wartime photograph of 1942 shows the basement windows bricked up.

The trumpet of war was still faint on the breeze when, on 28 June 1914, Archduke Franz Ferdinand, heir to the throne of Austria-Hungary, and his duchess were assassinated by a Serb nationalist in Sarajevo, Bosnia. This was the, almost inevitable, spark which set Europe alight and World War One was just days away. Austria-Hungary declared war on Serbia on 28 July, Russia mobilised in support of the Serbs so, on 1 August, Germany declared war on Russia. On 3 August Germany also declared war on France and then invaded Belgium on the way to the French border. It was the invasion of Belgium which brought Britain into the war, since she had agreed a treaty to protect Belgium's neutrality. No amount of diplomacy could prevent all-out war and at 11am on 4 August 1914 Prime Minister Asquith announced that Britain was now at war with Germany and her allies.

The effect of what would come to be known as the Great War was felt first at home. There was an immediate rush to buy food and supplies which took several weeks to subside, the hoarders sending prices soaring. Woodside Station became the hub of a supply route importing and exporting troops, transport and munitions. As many men volunteered to fight for their Empire, daily crowds of spectators and loved ones wished them fond farewells. When the Army commandeered the Oxton Carriage Co's horses for war service it left the company barely able to function.

On 19 August, German residents of Birkenhead were required to leave the town by Government order immediately. On 2 September the 'Pals' were formed and Birkenhead's commercial men and clerks joined 1,030 Liverpool and Wallasey commercial colleagues, to serve in a special battalion. It was reported that upwards of 30-40 men were rushing to the recruiting office in Market Street each hour.

On 5 September, Mackie and Gladstone, brewers of Birkenhead, were very concerned to advertise that their Amstel lager had been brewed in Amsterdam, presumably lest anyone assume its origins were German. The Mayoress, Mrs A.K. Arkle, set up the Belgian Relief Fund on 19 September 1914 to obtain funds for the distressed women and children who were refugees fleeing from German invaders. The Towers, an old mansion in Bebington Road, was assigned as the refugees' home. It was furnished, carpeted and victualled by local tradesmen and financed by charitable subscription collected by the Mayoress's fund. On 3 October, the refugees arrived in the town and were feted before being billeted.

At a recruiting drive in Liverpool on Monday 20 September, Mr Winston Churchill addressed potential servicemen and complimented his friend Mr F.E. Smith, who himself was off to war on 24 September. Meanwhile long queues, four deep, of women and children were to be seen waiting to receive aid at the Soldiers' and Sailors' Families' Association in Argyle Street. On 3 November, the doughty Bantam Battalion of recruits, too short for regular army service, attended a recruitment drive at Birkenhead Town Hall, their mascot a Bantam Cockerel. They were taken to a Bebington training camp. By the 12 December, C Company of the 14th Battalion Cheshire Regiment at Sandiway, Birkenhead had volunteered for service and were soon followed by six of the key male staff of Robb Brothers. But the war that everyone thought would be 'over by Christmas' was only just beginning and it would continue to influence and direct everyday life for some years to come.

Part 5

CHARITY AND SOCIAL IMPROVEMENT, ART AND EDUCATION.

GRAHAM WHITE AND THE LIBERALS UP TO 1939

1915, 1 January. The great resolution for the New Year: 'I will be a man and enlist today. At any Pay Office you can obtain the address of the nearest Recruiting Office. God Save the King!'

THE new year began much as the old one had ended, in a fervour of patriotism and optimism. But the enthusiasm Birkonians, like much of Britain, had for the war would soon wane when the first news drifted in from the front.

On 8 May 1915 came the first mention, in the *Birkenhead News,* of poisonous (chlorine) gas being used by the Germans in attacks on Allied soldiers. It came during the Second Battle of Ypres on 22 April, and in the Galicia actions, although both the German and French armies had used less dangerous, more irritant, chemical weapons earlier in the war. When large amounts of chlorine were ingested the gas caused slow and painful death by asphyxiation, though the almost immediate coughing it caused often limited the inhalation and saved many from death. But for those victims who did survive there was almost always permanent lung damage. As the war went on armies on both sides of the conflict discovered new forms of chemical weapons like phosgene and mustard gas that caused severe damage to unprotected skin and eyes. The British condemned the German use of the gas, while secretly preparing, and using, their own.

Further bad news from the war came on the afternoon of Friday 7 May 1915

BIRKENHEAD: AN ILLUSTRATED HISTORY

Della Robbia plaque, Central Library, Borough Road. Dedicated to the memory of Charles Gatehouse, deputy chairman of the Libraries committee 1898–1908.

when *RMS Lusitania* was torpedoed by German submarines off the Irish Coast with loss of 1,201 lives, including passengers, crew and three German stowaways locked in the cells. Among the dead were 128 US citizens, a fact which helped hasten the United States' entry into the war. Many local people were lost in the disaster including Miss Phyllis Hutchinson, 23 years, of Woodcroft, Bidston; Mr Charles Edwin Paynter of Oxton; Mr and Mrs Martin-Davey and their son Arthur of Caroline Place, Birkenhead; Mr McLeod, chief bedroom steward; and Mr Griffiths, ship's engineer, both of Old Chester Road, Birkenhead.

Two Tommies in France from the Harrowby Road group. The Harrowby Road Drill Hall was opened in 1907 as the Birkenhead HQ of the 1st Cheshire Royal Engineer Volunteers. In 1905 Lieutenant-Colonel Charles Brownridge, Borough Surveyor of Birkenhead became CO. He took part in the first Battle of Ypres in Autumn 1914.

On the 8 May, Saturday evening, in retaliation for the sinking, there were serious anti-German riots in Birkenhead. Anyone with a Germanic sounding name was vulnerable. Crowds gathered at the North End of Birkenhead. They began by stoning the butcher's shop of John Swarb in Watson Street. Charles Dashley's pork butchers shop was then vandalised by the angry crowd. and another of Mr Dashley's shops was attacked in Oxton Road and

A Charles Thompson picnic, 1915.

the property set alight. Police attempted to keep order but were overwhelmed. Many private houses were attacked. The occupants fled in fear of their lives. In Pilgrim Street many windows were smashed and barber's shops and grocer's shops in Oxton Road were broken into and looted. Mrs Gostenhofer's house in Waterford Street was the scene of an ugly demonstration. Many innocent people throughout the town were victimised due to their assumed German origins. At the police court the following Tuesday, the magistrate gave warning in consideration of one case of wilful damage. The only one of many that went untried. The magistrate said '...after making every allowance for the national indignation of one of the most awful crimes, we cannot allow you to take the law into your own hands. We hope there will be no repetition of these regrettable scenes.".

As May drew to a close the local papers continued to report more and more deaths at the front. Seven townspeople were named in the issue of 13 May alone. Lord Derby's special battalion, the Birkenhead Pals was serving in the trenches and experiencing a sad loss of life. But local newspapers reported that, despite this, they remained cheerful. The patriotic propaganda continued unabated but must surely have seemed ever more hollow as the full effects of the war became more clear.

Closer to home the townspeople had been saddened to hear of the death of Canon Andrew Knox of St Anne's, on 13 May. Canon Knox, champion of the poor and staunch supporter of Church-based education in the town, was mourned throughout the town. On 25 November 1917 Upton was to lose one of its most beloved and respected residents. The Very Revd Wilfred Canon Dallow, scion of the Roman Catholic Church and Rector to the Mission and Convent of St Joseph's for 35 years, died as a result of a motor accident. Canon Dallow, 70 years of age and well-loved throughout Birkenhead, had lived in the borough for 35 years helping all

A royal visit by King George V to Laird's on 14 May 1917. The war tonnage output was 152,108 tons.

George V making a tour of inspection at Laird's accompanied by Sir George Carter.

in the Roman Catholic community, and especially the poor at the North End of Birkenhead. His interest in history and archaeology influenced his search for and discovery of the Overchurch Runic Stones. The stones are now in Chester Museum.

Bad news from overseas would arrive on what seemed a daily basis and continued virtually for the duration of the war. On 7 June 1916 the town was rocked by the news that Lord Kitchener, regarded as a national hero for his overall command during the Boer War and later secretary of state for war, had been lost at sea off the Orkneys when his ship *HMS Hampshire* was sunk by German torpedoes en route to Russia. Knowing that military conscription would soon become necessary,

Birkenhead policewomen c.1917 at Bridewell Yard at the rear of the Town Hall.

Kitchener had begun the enlistment of thousands of men to arms and had appeared on recruitment posters declaring 'Your country needs YOU!' Though his ruthless tactics and single-minded determination forced his colleagues to relieve him of some of his responsibilities, Kitchener was worshiped by the British people and his death, shocking and sudden as it was, came as an enormous blow to public morale.

On the home front things were changing too. The war was creating food shortages on two fronts: merchant ships, bringing in vital supplies from the colonies and the United States, were often unable to reach the British Isles, and the ever-increasing number of men serving in the forces was taking workers away from farms causing an inevitable decrease in productivity. The Birkenhead master butchers held a meeting on 29 May to discuss meat shortages and the sudden increase in prices. They decided to close early, at 2pm, on Tuesday, Wednesday and Thursday. This would require customers to shop early, and to eke out supplies. It was hoped that the smaller market this would create would encourage wholesalers to reduce the price of the meat.

It was clear that the large numbers of men volunteering left a shortfall in the workforce that had to be filled – 'Women must work to fill the places of men at war!' was the rallying cry The Mayoress, Mrs A.H. Arkle, called a special meeting

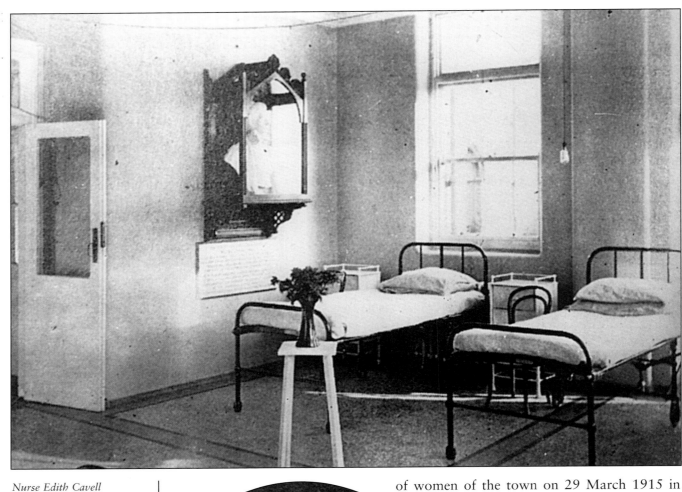

Nurse Edith Cavell Memorial Ward, Birkenhead Borough Hospital. The ward was funded by public subscription, inaugurated by the Birkenhead News, *and opened on 30 December 1918.*

Mrs Elizabeth Tutty, wife of Councillor Frederick Tutty, did valuable war work in World War One. She raised funds for the war effort, introducing tramways collections for the 'Penny Fund'. She also raised money through whist drives and sewing fêtes. Along with her husband, she managed the catering for Belgian refugees at The Towers, Victoria Park.

of women of the town on 29 March 1915 in which she asked them to support the President of the Board of Trade's appeal to the nation's women, whether they be skilled or unskilled. Naturally support was unanimous and the women of Birkenhead were on the march. For the first time women were employed as conductors on public tram-cars while others, like Miss Elsie Woodward delivered the post full-time, or were employed as street cleaners.

Modern Birkonians might imagine that, with the war occupying so many resources, both physical and emotional, that there would be little time for discontent. However, on 17 March 1915 employees of the gasworks went out on strike to campaign for an increase in wages. The situation was aggravated when the corporation elected to use the Bantam Volunteers' Battalion to protect gas supplies when heating and lighting were cut. At a time of great shortage, when many vital industrial processes – including the printing of the *Birkenhead News* – were under threat, strikers were stigmatised and regarded as unpatriotic for creating further problems at a time of national emergency.

The war and its tragedy was beginning to enshroud the town. Army and service hospitals for the wounded, centres for the recuperation of the war sick and rehabilitation centres were to open all over the town, many provided on a voluntary basis. In addition to the hospitals there were also several new reception centres to accept the wounded. Tranmere Military Infirmary was opened within St Catherine's Hospital when two blocks of the former workhouse infirmary were set aside and the borough hospital annex in Palm Grove was opened. Arrowe Hall was set aside as a hospital for the wounded and war veterans and Temple Road and Hemingford Road council schools were also converted to hospitals for the wounded. Abbotsford Red Cross Hospital was opened on 19 February 1916, thanks to Mr May Massey who had given his property to the War Office for the purpose. War casualties began to pour into the town. On 8 July 1916, 350 wounded soldiers arrived at Woodside Station. They were taken to Hemingford Road School Hospital.

The local paper now featured a special section entitled 'Our Patriots' in which the dead and wounded were honoured. It was full of headlines like 'Died like a man', 'St Mary's Old Boy Falls', 'Glorious Death', 'Another Cheshire Fallen', the headlines were unending.

The first branch maternity and child welfare clinic at Brassey Street Mission premises. The opening ceremony, seen here, was performed in 1919.

Unloading country produce at Birkenhead Market c.1919.

Williamson Art Gallery, Birkenhead, opened 1928 and donated by John Williamson, JP and his son Patrick.

With so many men falling victim it had, by July 1915, become necessary to enforce conscription. Zeppelin Bombing Raids were also now a constant fear and, as a consequence, the Government announced a compulsory blackout. All houses and other buildings were forbidden to allow even a chink of light to escape into the darkened street for fear of giving the Zeppelin pilots a target to aim their bombs at. Rostances' haberdashery, at 169-173 Old Chester Road, sold blackout window blinds to assist the effort. Additionally, buckets of water and sand were to be kept ready to quench fires in upper rooms, whilst all windows and doors were to be kept closed on ground floors.

There were, of course, attempts at maintaining normality within the town. Tranmere Rovers Football Club kept Birkonian spirits on the rise by beating local rivals Altrincham at home in October 1916.

W.W. Kelly's new Theatre Royal also kept the townsfolk entertained throughout the war, presenting Ibsen's *Ghosts* in May 1917 (to adult audiences only) and George Bernard Shaw's *Pygmalion* in October the same year. The Royal National Eisteddfod of Wales was held in Birkenhead Park in September 1917. In December the Honourary Secretary was given permission to retain the stones of the Gorsedd, used at the festival, in the grounds of the park. It was a significant compliment to the faithful Welsh community of the town, matched only by the council's own

honour in conferring the freedom of Birkenhead on Mr David Lloyd George, the Prime Minister when he had visited the Eisteddfod on 5-7 September 1917.

Exhibits at the Williamson Gallery: The Wreck of the Birkenhead, *1852. A 1922 oil on canvas by Thomas M. Hemy (1852–1937).* The Grove, Bridgnorth, *1911 oil on canvas by Philip Wilson Steer (1860–1942)*

The tragic death of Edith Cavell, was mourned across the country. An English nurse, who had remained in charge of a hospital in Brussels after the German occupation, she assisted Allied troops to escape to Holland. Having helped more than 200 men to freedom, she was arrested for espionage by the Germans and executed late in 1915. She was regarded as nothing less than a martyr. In her memory the Mayoress of Birkenhead, helped by the editor of the *Birkenhead News*, established a fund to finance the foundation of the Edith Cavell Memorial Ward in Birkenhead Borough Hospital. The fund already a great success by December 1915. Edith Cavell's sacrifice was a perfect example to inspire the townspeople. The fund continued until 1918 when the memorial ward was opened.

On 22 July 1916 'our wounded heroes' were celebrated with a 'sacred concert' at

Masanielle (or 'Neapolitan fisher boy'). Presented to the Williamson Art Gallery by Alfred Holt Esq, of the famous shipping company, in October 1930. It was transferred to the new Birkenhead Central Library on 29 June 1934 as a fitting centrepiece for the entrance hall, doubtless due to the nautical associations of the statue and the geographical location. Masanielle (1620–1647) led an insurrection against Spanish nobles of Florence and was later assasinated by them. The sculpture is white marble on a green marble base, intricately carved with fish and nets. The sculptor was Italian Augusto Passaglia (1838–1918).

the Theatre Royal in Argyle Street, arranged by the Birkenhead Police and Tradesmen's Charity Committee.

On 18 December Birkenhead received the congratulations of the National War Savings Committee when it ranked first of County boroughs with 100 different war savings organisations.

King George V and Queen Mary returned to Birkenhead on 14 May 1917 and toured Cammell Laird's yard to express thanks to shipyard workers for their dedicated efforts.

However, raising the town's morale was exceptionally difficult when every issue of the local paper published a roll of honour – men killed, wounded or missing in battle, each one longer than the previous issue's.

The *Birkenhead News* of 18 November 1917, published a group photograph of Birkenhead men of the Cheshire Regiment who took part in the capture of Baghdad. These men had been through the Mesopotamian campaign, the attempted relief at Kut and the futile struggle in Gallipoli. Rightly so, these men were lauded as heroes.

The crimson ribbon of the Victoria Cross was worn by Birkenhead's valourous Riflemen A.H. Proctor when he was married to Miss Hilda Dodd at St Paul's Church, Tranmere on 23 May 1917. The medal was conferred on 16 August 1916 for conspicuous gallantry in saving his comrades of the Liverpool Regiment at the front whilst under heavy artillery fire. The King invested Rifleman Proctor on the battlefield during his visit to the men serving in France.

At a more sombre ceremony in St Paul's Churchyard, on 5 August 1917, the Mayor Mr James Merritt had unveiled Birkenhead's first shrine to the fallen of the parish.

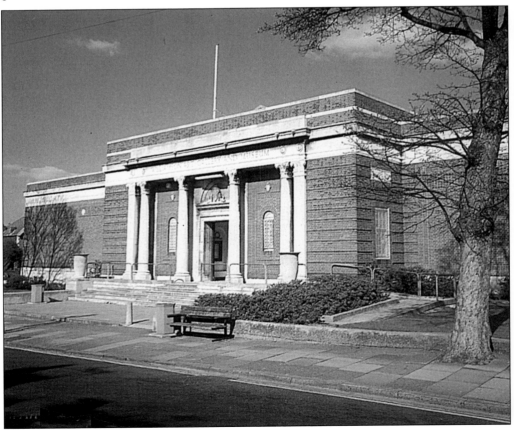

Williamson Art Gallery and Museum.

It was fitting that in the last days of 1917, Miss Helen Ryder, Sister in Command of the Mersey Park Military Hospital was invested with the Royal Red Cross by George V. Her 20 years service on behalf of the wounded, her service at war in France when she cared for the wounded whilst under bombardment and at risk to her life, all merited the honour she received.

In the New Year's Honours of 1918, two notable Birkonians were listed. Firstly noted politician, the Right Honourable Sir F.E. Smith, KC, MP, was created a baronet. He had served with the Oxford Yeomanry at the front. Equally well-known in the town was the Right Honourable Ellis J. Griffith KC, MP, a former recorder of Birkenhead who was also created baronet. He served the borough from 1907–12, was elected to the Bar in 1887, had a successful political career and became Secretary of State for the Home Department in 1915.

While the war raged on, domestic matters were still of great importance. In October 1917, Mr H. Graham White of Mere Cottage, Oxton was selected by the Executive of the Birkenhead Liberal Association as one of the two candidates for the borough at the next General Election, although his family had a long history in the Conservative movement. Graham White was already a councillor, for Egerton, and keenly interested in helping boy's organisations. He served as a governor of Birkenhead School, the Birkenhead Institute and the Albert Memorial Industrial School. He had served on education, libraries and ferries committees for the borough. His paramount intention in 1917 was to bring the war to a successful conclusion and then to obtain the greatest good for the greatest number of the Birkenhead population.

On 5 December 1917 Birkenhead's first female councillor was elected. Miss Annie Laird was unanimously chosen for the Oxton Ward seat vacated by Mr David MacIver. Alderman Arkle paid tribute to all the women of the town, who had thrown themselves into the breach created by the war years and particularly congratulated Miss Laird as a most suitable first woman councillor carrying on the traditions set down by her famous forbears of the town. The alderman also praised the foresight of

Captain A.C. Dawson, Chief Constable 1923–42.

Visit of HRH Princess Mary, Viscountess Lascelles, to Cammell Laird on 17 December 1925 to launch HMS Rodney.

Argyle Theatre, Birkenhead, the stage, a 1920s view.

Government in proposing that women be enfranchised. It would prove an historic day for the town.

Wartime saw the introduction of a number of facilities aimed at the children of the borough. The now flourishing Boy Scout movement in the town was again honoured when Baden-Powell reviewed the Scouts and Girl Guides at Birkenhead Park. The future men of Birkenhead were so honoured on 1 December 1917 when a Newsboy's Social Club was started in the town at the cost of *Liverpool Daily Post and Echo* in premises in Grange Road. This was to provide recreation for poor boys of the town who had nowhere to go after their news deliveries. Mr Jones of the *Echo* and Mr Worrall of the *Birkenhead News* would organise games, physical exercise, concerts, lectures and sport to keep boys off the streets and happily occupied. That year at Christmas, Charles Thompson's Poor Children's Mission in Hemingford Street, served 1,000 Christmas dinners at six sittings in three eating halls and, after all the children had been fed, the widows and poor mothers were also given a meal. Afterwards Miss Annie Thompson and Mr Charles Thompson distributed hundreds of toys and provided entertainment. Although much development had been postponed due to the intervention of hostilities, World War One had proved a catalyst for many social changes.

The war finally drew to a close on 11 November 1918, on what would become Armistice Day. The mayor, Mr D.R. Rowlands, announced the end of hostilities at an impromptu thanksgiving in Hamilton Square in front of a huge crowd. He said that hearts were too full for them to voice the sentiments that filled their souls.It would be some time before the appalling suffering and wholesale slaughter, that had been so characteristic of World War One, would become apparent. The first understanding, of course, would come when the soldiers returned from the trenches, and also in the poetry which so many of them wrote. One of the most famous war poets was Wilfred Owen who, though born in Shrewsbury in 1893, had lived in Birkenhead between 1898 until 1907 when his father took a post with the Birkenhead to Chester Railway. Wilfred was educated at Birkenhead Institute but had returned to Shrewsbury and attended Shrewsbury Technical School in 1907. He taught English in Bordeaux and the Pyrenees. In 1915 he joined up and was eventually commissioned with the Manchester Regiment 5th (Reserve) Battalion. By 1918 he had served two years – a hard and terrible time at the front – and suffered

Woodside during the General Strike of 1926.

shellshock, a condition which would probably be termed post-traumatic stress disorder today. After a period in hospital, he rejoined his regiment and went back into action. On 4 November, Owen was killed in action, shot at Hancourt.

His poetry lived on beyond his death and the deaths of so many of his contemporaries.

He wrote:

'Red lips are not so red

As the stained stones of the English dead.'

Wilfred Owen is commemorated in Birkenhead with a decorative window that bursts over the main staircase of the Birkenhead Central Library.

With peacetime came more changes and rapid development. A General Election was arranged for December 1918 and Birkenhead was now divided into two constituencies – Birkenhead East and Birkenhead West.

The result was in favour of the Coalition Unionists and Mr A.H. Bigland and Lieutenant-Colonel H.M. Grayson were elected. Mr H. Graham White (Liberal) was not, on this occasion, successful. Lord Birkenhead was elected in West Derby and after a month was invited by Prime Minister David Lloyd George to preside as Lord Chancellor.

In 1919 Birkenhead adopted motor bus services for the town. The first route was from Rock Ferry to Moreton and was an immediate success. By 1938, the tram service was completely replaced by modern motor buses. A gaily illuminated

Arrowe Hall. Built in 1835, with subsequent extensions, the hall was purchased by Birkenhead Corporation from Lord Leverhulme in 1926.

tramcar made the last journey on the last remaining route – Oxton and Claughton Circle.

The population census of 1921 showed an increase of 16,783 persons in the town. That same year the new water supply from Alwen Reservoir was inaugurated. In 1928 the borough expanded to include the ancient and holy parish of Landican (Land chene); the former meeting ground and Parliament of the early Danish settlers in the Wirral at Thingwall; Prenton Township and the Earl of Derby's Bidston Manor and Village. The borough boundaries were further extended in 1933 with the additions of parishes Noctorum, Woodchurch, Arrowe and Upton. The docks were also extended to include Bidston Dock.

In 1922, the New Ferry Cross River Service, a branch of the Birkenhead Corporation Ferry Service, which had been inaugurated in 1865 to facilitate the wealthy merchant residents of New Ferry, was closed down, so reducing Birkenhead ferry services at a time of financial slump and high unemployment. This was something of a foretaste of the future and, in 1925, work was commenced on the building of the Mersey Tunnel from Birkenhead to Liverpool – a joint venture for the town and the city. The tunnel was completed in 1934 and was opened by the King on 18 July. The mammoth excavations and building work had taken nine years. Pilot headings had to be driven under the river from Liverpool and Birkenhead. In March 1928 the two sides met when 'break through' was achieved.

The Lord Mayor of Liverpool and the Mayor of Birkenhead marked the occasion on 3 April when they shook hands across the opening. The 2.13 mile long road work was undertaken by Sir Basil Motte and J.A. Brodie the engineers of the 2.13 mile.

The architect, Herbert J. Rowse, designed the main entrances, lodges, approach roads, pay booths and retaining walls. The materials, Portland stone and polished black granite were skillfully used to follow the styles reminiscent of Egyptian pyramids and pharoahs' tombs. The design reflected an enthusiasm for all things exotic that was the very essence of what has since become known as Art Deco. Clean lines and bold structures were being erected across the globe from Bombay to Birkenhead. These buildings were usually decorated with motifs borrowed from distant cultures reflecting the new explorers who were bringing back decorative treasures from around the world. Egyptian motifs like these were the height of fashion thanks to Howard Carter's recent excavations of Tutankhamun's tomb from 1922–4. At the centre of the Birkenhead Tunnel approach, a 60ft obelisk of black granite, heavily fluted with a decorative head, flower-like and illuminated stood as a grand centre-piece. There is also a smaller dock entrance in Rendel Street similar in style. The ventilation stations of the tunnel are also impressive. Again Art Deco with Egyptian details, there are three of these tall brick structures at strategic points – close to the river at Woodside, Sidney Street and Taylor Street. Anything and everything electrically powered was also highly fashionable so it was fitting that George V should use an electrical switch to open the Liverpool and Birkenhead tunnel entrances simultaneously. The ceremony took place at the Liverpool Entrance and the King and Queen then drove through the tunnel to Birkenhead, where His Majesty opened the magnificent new Central Library, again by use of an electrical switch.

The Central Library was the pride of the Birkenhead Library Service, which had proved highly popular and very successful since first adopted in 1856. The first Central Library in Hamilton Street (built 1864), outgrew its usefulness and was replaced by a grand new building in Market Place South in 1909, financed in part by the philanthropist Andrew Carnegie. It was a disappointment in 1929 when the Mersey Joint Tunnel Committee chose to acquire the library site for the entrance to the new road tunnel. Compensation of £55,000 was allowed for an ambitious new building sited on the main Borough Road.

The design was to be decided by holding a competition. Gray, Evans and Crossley won the commission and built a gleaming, white stone, Neo-Georgian palace with imposing pillared portico, incorporating a balcony. The landscaped frontage had steps leading up from the roadway. Inside, the best Carrara marble and English oak were used. The workmanship of the furniture and fittings was of the very finest quality. The Lending Department

Bidston Hall. This was the 6th Earl of Derby's hunting lodge, dating from c.1620. In 1928 the Birkenhead boundaries were extended to include Bidston.

Y. M. C. A., BIRKENHEAD.

11th January, 1908.

Dear Sir,

You may be interested to know that

Lieutenant=General Baden=Powell, C.B.,

has very kindly consented to give a Lecture, illustrated with Lime-light Views, in our Hall, on

FRIDAY, JANUARY 24th, 1908.

The subject of his lecture will be

"Scouting and Good Citizenship,"

it being the explanation of a scheme for instructing boys in Scouting, and an appeal for men to help in carrying out the same in Birkenhead.

SIR JOHN GRAY HILL

will occupy the chair at 8-30, and the Committee would be greatly obliged if you could be present. The tickets for admission will be 1/- and 6d., but Reserved Seats at 2/- each can be obtained at the Y.M.C.A. prior to the day of the Lecture.

Yours faithfully,

W. H. RALSTON,

General Secretary.

A 1908 programme detailing a visit to Birkenhead of Robert Baden-Powell.

Twenty-one years after the inauguration of the Boy Scout movement in Birkenhead at the YMCA building on Grange Road, Sir Robert Baden-Powell celebrated the International Scout Jamboree at Arrowe Park from 31 July–12 August 1929. The Prince of Wales attended. This is the great Scout leader's official jamboree portrait.

featured plaques by the Della Robbia pottery on the walls in memory of Charles Gatehouse, chairman of the Libraries Committee, removed from the previous library. A marble bust of William Shakespeare was given a place on the first-floor landing, a gift of the Birkenhead Literary and Scientific Society in 1864, on the 300th anniversary of the playwright's birth. Likewise, this sculpture has been moved from library to library since 1864, with its accompanying specialist collection of books on Shakespeare. The library boasted a valuable collection of fine and antiquarian books including a copy of the *Nuremberg Chronicle* of 1483. The entrance hall holds a gleaming statue, *Masaniello* by Passaglia, representing maritime Birkenhead and presented by Alfred Holt, shipping magnate. A work apt for the town, since Masaniello, a 17th century Neopolitan fisherman, had been a rebellious champion of the poor of Naples.

On 5 July 1925 Lieutenant-General Sir Richard H.K. Butler unveiled Birkenhead's war memorial in Hamilton Square. The monument to the memory of 1,293 Birkenhead men who fell in World War One is of simple classical design, according to guidelines laid down for the production of appropriate sacred monuments, both in economy and simplicity. Lionel Budden, architect of Birkenhead and Liverpool carried out the work with sculpture decoration by H. Tyson Smith. 20,000 people watched the ceremony on the four sides of the square in sorrowful attendance.

Thirteen months later, in August 1926 Birkenhead Corporation purchased Arrowe Hall and Park from Lord Leverhulme, who had acquired it in 1908. The neo-Elizabethan hall, originally built in 1835 and designed by John Cunningham for John Ralph Shaw of the shipping family, Shaw Savill Line, stood in 425 acres of grounds. It proved an ideal park for Birkenhead. The grounds contained an 18 hole golf course, regarded as a necessary luxury in the 1920s and 1930s.

On 1 December 1928, Birkenhead's cultural centre, the Williamson Art Gallery and Museum, was opened. This purpose-built gallery, with special equipment for preservation of art-work and artefacts, was given to the town by John Williamson, a director of the Cunard shipping line. A previous gallery had been opened in the old Central Library in Hamilton Street and, due to the far-sighted policy undertaken in the first art gallery, several specialised collections have now become associated with the Williamson. Of particular importance is the maritime collection. A piece of considerable poignancy is Hemy's cartoon of the *Wreck of the Birkenhead*. The frigate *Birkenhead*, built by Laird's in 1846, sailed from Wallasey Pool on her way to the Cape of Good Hope, carrying troops and their dependent wives and children. The ship was taking reinforcements to the army at the time of the Eighth Kaffir War. On 26 February 1852, she struck a rock off Cape Town and sank in just 25 minutes. The soldiers lined the decks in formation to stand fast allowing the women and children to escape first in the boats, 193 persons were saved, 445 men were drowned or taken by sharks. Their heroic discipline will always be remembered – the dramatic picture is just one memorial to the event.

The gallery holds a comprehensive collection of English watercolours, including paintings by Edward Cox, Thomas Girtin the 'King of Watercolour', John Sell Cotman, David Cox and Peter de Wint. Of oil paintings there are many fine examples like W.C. Penn's *Head of a Negro* and *Lamorna Cove* by local artist S.J. Lamorna Birch RA. There is also a near-complete collection of the works of P. Wilson Steer, who was born in Birkenhead in 1860. He studied at Gloucester Art School where he was taught by John Kemp. Later he went to Paris and was very much influenced by Degas. He is considered to be one of the most distinguished

The World Jamboree Memorial, Arrowe Park. Presented by the Scout Association to the Borough of Birkenhead in 1929.

Birkenhead Park CC, 1st XI 1931 season. Back row (left to right): E.S. Chantrell, F.C. Cockle, N. Carter, G.H. Ferns, D.H. Brabner, Bartley, J.H. Rogers, W. Coglan (umpire). Front row: H.W. Hodgson, Hartley E. Smith (president), A.R. Crooke, J.H. Rogers (vice-president), J.P. Hodgson. Seated on ground: C.W. Timmins, J.C.G. Tilby.

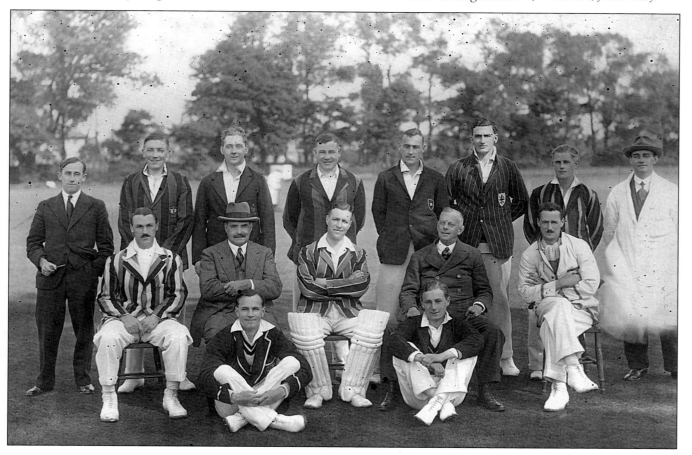

George Stratton Esq,
FRSA, ALA, AMA. Chief
Librarian and Curator,
County Borough of
Birkenhead from 1922–69.

British landscape artists. Among his oil paintings is *The Muslin Dress*, 1910. His watercolours include many landscapes of Dover, Shoreham and Richmond. Steer was awarded the Order of Merit in 1931. He died on 21 March 1942.

The Williamson ceramics collection is vast and covers examples of the best of leading English factories from Wedgewood, Derby, Spode and Copeland to the local wares of Liverpool's Herculaneum Pottery and Seacombe Pottery. Continental wares are also on show such as Sevre's vases of 1756. A Copenhagen Flora Danica Service and a Swan Vase. There are also examples of Japanese and Chinese porcelain. The sculpture collection includes many oriental bronzes and glass wares dating back several centuries. The Gallery cherishes a unique collection of the Della Robbia pottery which was established by Harold Rathbone in his home at 21, Hamilton Square in 1894. Harold was the son of the wealthy Liverpool family which had influence in the city and in the arts world, particularly at the Walker Art Gallery. First and foremost, Rathbone was an artist, a businessman second. But he realised that there was a profitable market for fine art works amongst the wealthy residents of Birkenhead. He had travelled in Italy and France and had trained at the Slade spending much time with several artist contemporaries. William Morris, Ford Madox Brown and the Pre-Raphaelites were an influence on his work and he became involved in the Arts and Crafts Movement of the late 1890s. He believed that everyone had unique artistic creativity which might be encouraged and developed and was to encourage many unknowns with great success.

The frontage of Birkenhead Central Library, Borough Road, summer 1994, 60 years after it was opened by King George V, on 18 July 1934.

Rathbone admired the work of the 15th-century sculptor, Luca Della Robbia and so adopted the name for his pottery works. Artists in his employ included his co-founder Dressler, sculptor Manzoni, Cassandia Anne Walker, John Bowers and Liz Wilkins. Clients were often distinguished and included Queen Victoria, the Prince and Princess of Wales, and the Mayor of Birkenhead, Edward George Mason, for whom he fashioned the Mason Vase.

Many Della Robbia pieces decorate local buildings, as in Birkenhead Central Library, a piece entitled *To Walk Humbly With Thy God* consisting of a series of ceramic decorations in the Memorial Church, Manor Road, Wallasey. In 1906 Rathbone closed down his factory, dissatisfied with its profits. Many of the workers were local people and they received a gift of their choice of piece in payment for their loyalty. In the interceding years a large collection of Della Robbia has been acquired by the Art Gallery.

The gallery's tapestry room is a memorial to another member of Birkenhead's rich heritage of creative thinkers. This was Arthur H. Lee whose jacquard weaving business opened in Stanley Road in 1908. The tapestry works, or Tap as it was known in the docklands and poor areas of Birkenhead stood adjacent to dock workers cottages. The Tap benefited from nearby sea, rail and motor supply routes to easily transport the finished product to buyers across the country. In more recent years the Williamson Art Gallery became the local Arts Centre where organisations might meet and hold exhibitions. The gallery continues to go from strength to strength, brightening the lives of Birkonians.

An event which not only brought great celebration to Birkenhead but which also gave the town a great deal of pride was the 1929 World Scout Jamboree which was held at Arrowe Park in July and August. The opening ceremony, on 31 July, was performed by HRH the Duke of Connaught, the King's uncle. HRH the Prince of Wales arrived at the Jamboree on 1 August and, representing his father the King, toured the camp before leaving the next day. So many scouts and their leaders attended what was described as the 'Coming of Age Jamboree', celebrating 21 years of scouting, that a campsite one mile by half a mile was needed. Some reports suggested that 56,000 scouts from countries far and wide had attended like those from India, where the scouts had had to walk a hundred miles through mountain and jungle to reach the railhead. It was reported that the German contingent had hiked all the way from Grimsby, and that many British scouts had walked many miles because they could not afford the train fare. Some 1,500 American scouts marching behind the Stars and Stripes mingled with scouts from the corners of the Empire. Each group enacted scenes from their history or traditional dances, songs and stories. There were camp-fire sing-songs, shows and games and the camp newspaper, the *Daily Arrowe* sold more than 30,000 copies daily. The Chief Scout Baden-Powell was presented with a portrait of himself by David Jagger and, at the closing ceremony, following 14 days of celebration, he addressed the attendees.

'From all corners of the earth you have journeyed to this great gathering of world fellowship and brotherhood. Today I send you out from Arrowe to all the World,

On the same visit to Birkenhead the King opened the Birkenhead Tunnel under the Mersey. He is accompanied by Queen Mary, with the Earl of Derby, far right.

bearing my symbol of peace and fellowship, each one of you my ambassador, bearing my message of love and fellowship on the wings of sacrifice and service, to the ends of the earth. From now on, the Scout symbol of Peace is the Golden Arrow. Carry it fast and far, so that all men may know the brotherhood of man.'

Four golden arrows were issued, one for each point of the compass, and they were taken back home by some of the visiting scout groups.

Despite these glorious occasions, the lot of the average Birkonian was less than comfortable. As many as 1,120 families out of 7,000 were living below the poverty line which accounted for 15 percent of the Birkenhead population. Of these, one out of every four families was forced to share a house. The 1920s and 30s saw a lull in trade and commerce, with consequent rise in unemployment. National Assistance was very small and many families suffered extreme poverty. One in three people was without work. Most dockers at this time worked three days and then spent three days on the dole. Long queues from the Labour Exchange in Bridge Street stretched to Hamilton Square every day. Unemployment Benefit was only granted after taking the means test, a harsh and humiliating exercise. An inspector from the Public Assistance Committee would visit the applicant's home. If there were private possessions, these must be sold before benefit could be received. Pawnshops and wardrobe dealers had long queues at the doors all day. Mothers would take up charring (cleaning) work or take in washing. Pay was minimal. During 1932, 526 children were reported as being badly clad and received clothes from the Police Benevolent Fund. Dinner tickets for free meals were given to very poor children.

Morale was rock bottom. Many unemployed people attempted suicide. Many were vilified as workshy loafers. Many would go to the library just to keep warm,

Inside the Queensway Mersey Tunnel, 1934.

A panoramic view of the opening ceremony of the Queensway Mersey Tunnel.

The launching of the 22,000-ton aircraft carrier HMS Ark Royal, 13 April 1937. The ship was launched by Lady Maude Hoare. after four attempts to smash the bottle and an exhortation from the workforce to 'Give it to Dixie!' Birkenhead-born Dixie Dean had been scoring goals for Everton for more than a decade by then, after beginning his career at Tranmere Rovers.

and occupy their time in reading books and newspapers. There were many premature deaths due to unfit, hungry men taking on heavy work. When construction began on the Mersey Tunnel in the mid-1920s an unusually high number of labourers suffered heart attacks.

In 1919, Birkenhead Police had taken strike action for better pay and working conditions. The strike lasted a fortnight during which there was looting and mob-rule in the town. 500 troops were called in to restore order until the force received new pay scales and resumed duty.

That riotous element simmered on until, in 1932, they resumed in earnest in Bryanston Road; outside the Board of Guardians Office in Conway Street and in various sites on Price Street and the poorer districts of town. The 15 and 16 September 1932 were marked with vicious rioting, with meetings at Birkenhead Park, marches to Hamilton Square, looting and vandalism in Grange Road and in Price Street. Rioting continued in the town up to 19 September, when the Public Assistance Committee, Conservative town council and the chief constable called a truce with the demonstrators. Thirty-one men had been arrested and refused bail, but crowds of unemployed men gathered in Argyle Street and were joined by workers, leaving their shifts, their wives and friends. The chief constable was in fear of a repeat of the mob's retaliation ravages when the troops entered Birkenhead at the General Strike of 1926. The damage to his and the council's reputation would be severe. The solution gave success to the unemployed when their relief was raised at the committee's meeting at 4.30pm. Single men were granted 15s 3d; single

women – 13s 6d, and work schemes to the value of £170,000 were to be introduced. Finally it was at least a measure of victory for the unemployed. There were repercussions throughout the country and riots were mentioned in Parliament on 19 October by Sir Stafford Cripps, who took sides with the unemployed, persuading Prime Minister Ramsay MacDonald to review the means test in the following week.

Arthur Lee's tapestry works at one time employed over 500 people. The different tasks – dyeing, card-cutting and weaving warranted a varied scale of wages and each had its accompanying dangers – flying shuttles, splashing acids, steamy dye house atmosphere and extreme noise in the weaving shed. Nevertheless the continued success of Lee's was a job-seeker's godsend. The atmosphere was friendly and staff took pride in making beautiful items for some of the finest homes and businesses in the world. Over the years tapestries and fabrics were made for luxury liners like the *RMS Queen Mary* and the *RMS Strathmore* and for fine houses, banks and boardrooms. Some of the wealthiest and most influential people in the world sought it out. First Lady Jacqueline Kennedy ordered items for the White House; Prime Minister Harold Wilson made purchases for 10 Downing Street; the Sheik of Kuwait had 1,200,000 stitches of petit-point wall hanging for his palace.

The Lees were good to their staff and performed many good works for the underprivileged people who lived near their works. The girls they employed gave good financial support to their unemployed parents and local poor children were taken to Dyserth Holiday Camp by the firm and looked after by the staff. In 1909, Arthur Lee had begun the Merseyside Holiday Camps for poor kids and, on

Car No.42 was decorated to mark the last week of tramway operation in July 1937. Trams are back at Woodside Ferry as part of the Woodside Heritage Trail. This is not a branch of the official transport service.

Top left: Launch of the RMS Mauretania, 28 July 1938. Lady Bates is pictured unveiling the name on the bows of the ship.

Top right: Advertisement of 1939 promoting the Mauretania.

Wednesday nights, he would organise regular slide shows and entertainment for the boys and girls of the Dock Cottages. There were also Christmas parties for the local people with a tree and presents.

Tap survived World War Two and many important commissions were honoured. But mass production of textiles and patterned fabrics began to compete with Lee's for prime orders and the business began to fall off until the works was closed in August 1970.

RMS Mauretania, *built at Birkenhead.*

The Williamson Art Gallery acquired many of the artefacts of the factory and, together with patterns, a loom, photographs and documents, now provides an archive repository for one of the most intriguing artistic enterprises of Birkenhead's culture.

Local art and painting is well represented in the gallery, with a collection of Liverpool School of Painters 1810–67. George Stubbs, Samuel Austin and William Davis (Davis of Liverpool) are just three of the many artists represented.

Birkenhead enjoyed a brief boom in the 1920s when Cammell Laird won orders for

Leading stoker Walter Arnold and Mr Frank Shaw, engine-fitter of Cammell Laird, July 1939. Survivors of the Thetis *tragedy, both men were from Birkenhead.*

Launching of HMS Thetis *at Cammell Laird yard on 29 June 1938.*

new ships *RMS Fullagar* and *HMS Rodney*. In 1928 the Alfred Dock Entrance Lock was opened by Lord Derby, but for most the situation remained dire. During the depths of the Depression Cammell Laird saw their order books reduced to one ship and the workforce was reduced to 2,000 labourers. In the mid-1930s business began to pick up. *HMS Ark Royal* was a Laird's commission and launched in 1937. This was followed by the *RMS Mauritania* for the Cunard Line in 1938 – the biggest merchant ship built in England – and in May 1939 royalty again visited Cammell Laird, when Mary, the Princess Royal came to Birkenhead to launch *HMS Prince of Wales*. Of course this new relative prosperity eventually filtered through to the working man and woman, but whilst the dark skies over the economy might be lightening, the black clouds of war were bubbling up in Europe once more. It didn't escape notice, of course, that the full order book was largely the result of the Royal Navy strengthening its fleet.

But even before the declaration of war tragedy was to come to Birkenhead. On 1 June 1939 the submarine *HMS Thetis*, launched from the Cammell Laird yards on 29 June 1938, went on diving trials in the Liverpool Bay. Five hours later she was lying 160 feet down on the bottom of the bay, with her bow in the mud. A final coat of paint had blocked a vital valve giving the false reading that a torpedo tube was dry when it was, in fact, full of water. An internal torpedo tube door was opened, water gushed in and *Thetis* sank. Part of the *Thetis* remained above water for two hours and she was only 38 miles from land, but of the 103 men who sailed in her, a mere four survived. A somewhat inexpert rescue operation, little survival training, and an unfortunate chain of events left the submariners to their deaths. A pall settled over Birkenhead during the frantic, but ill-fated attempts to bring the *Thetis* and her

The memorial to HMS Thetis *at Holyhead, unveiled and dedicated 7 November 1947.*

A weaver busy at her loom at A.H. Lee & Sons.

crew to the surface. At 4.10pm on Saturday 3 June, a statement was issued from Whitehall.

'The Admiralty regrets that hope of saving lives in the *Thetis* must be abandoned.'

Towards the end of August, attempts to salvage the submarine, and retrieve the bodies of her crew claimed another victim when one of the rescue divers suffered a fatal attack of the bends.

Due to the urgency of the situation during the early months of World War Two, the *Thetis* was repaired and recommissioned as *HMS Thunderbolt*. *Thunderbolt* served in the Battle of the Atlantic but was sunk by an Italian ship in the Mediterranean Sea.

Ten weeks after the loss of the *Thetis*, the escalating tensions in Europe had come to a head. Adolf Hitler had defied warnings to cease his ruthless expansion of Nazi Germany and, on 3 September 1939 at 11.15am, Prime Minister Neville Chamberlain announced in a broadcast to the nation that Britain was at war with Germany. It had been so short a time since the end of the 'war to end all wars' that gloom, despondency and fear infiltrated the county immediately. For several weeks plans had been under way to prepare for war. In Birkenhead, the council formed war committees to meet the emergencies and carry out vital functions. The Food Central Committee started food rationing in September. Fresh memories of World War One shortages made provision of adequate food and nutrition a priority. The Communal Feeding Committee organised several British Restaurants in the town. An Air Raid Precautions Committee had plans for shelters and air-raid warnings, in the event of bombings or gas attacks. The Emergency Committee was responsible for dealing with any war damage. The town was on alert.

Tapestry weaving by Jacquard power loom, A.H. Lee & Sons Ltd, 1940.

Part 6

WAR, TRAGEDY, DOCK STRIKES, GLORIOUS MOMENTS TO 1974

BY the time 1940 arrived air-raid sirens, barrage balloons, Anderson shelters, emergency water supply tanks and gas masks were the order of the day. On Merseyside air-raid sirens, which soon became known as moaning minnies, had sounded for the first time on 25 June 1940. The alert came after midnight when German planes were heard but not sighted. In Birkenhead the first bombing raid came at 12:30am on 9 August 1940 when a series of high-explosive bombs fell on Prenton. One penetrated the roof of a house at Pine Walks, Prenton, killing a maid. The house belonged to Mr Ernest Henry Bunny, a notable Birkenhead resident and owner of the family business, Bunny's household stores, in Church Street, Liverpool. From this date onward, until May the following year, at least one serious German bombing raid came per month, shattering Birkenhead, and killing in total 382 people and leaving 606 seriously injured.

The Nazis were intent on disabling shipyards and the industry of the port as well as breaking the spirit of the people. From September 1940 there were daily and nightly raids on the dockland areas and their residents. Birkenhead was getting used to the idea that it was in the front line.

On 6 September the Birkenhead Children's Convalescent Home was hit and later that month there was a number of 'sharp' raids. On 27 September the Argyle Theatre was gutted, yet in the corpse of the world-famous building, Mr Tom Clarke ran up a defiant Union Flag on the surviving tower. For months now radio listeners had been subjected to the mocking tones of 'Lord Haw Haw' – the British traitor William Joyce who played an important part in the Nazi propaganda war. His broadcasts which began 'Germany calling! Germany calling!' always warned of the horrors to come, their intention to break the spirit of the British people. This time Lord Haw Haw foretold: 'The people of Birkenhead may sit on the their ruins and watch Liverpool burn.' And so it proved – a greater attack than ever before engulfed Liverpool on 28 November. And then, on 20 December, began even heavier raids of high-explosives and incendiaries. Birkenhead dockside warehouses and railways

Argyle Theatre, Birkenhead bomb damage in September 1940.

were badly damaged. The Church of Our Lady on Corporation Road was bombed, the presbytery receiving a direct hit which killed Canon Tallon, a well-known Birkenhead priest.

In the raids of 12/13 March 1941, the properties on both sides of Borough Road were razed to the ground and a tragic 288 men, women and children lost their lives. Out of 34,000 dwellings, over 25,000 were damaged, over 1,600 were hit as many as three times, and 7,500 residents had to be evacuated.

Civilians in the civil defence and fire services were heroic. Of the wardens and WVS, 28 were killed and 14 injured in one night alone during May. Although the May Blitz was exceptional, the enemy's main objective had not been achieved, for the port continued to function normally. Even the horrendous Mersey explosion of the *Malakand*, part of the Brocklebank line, a 7,649-ton freighter in Huskisson Dock at 11.15pm on 3 May – an explosion which sent shock waves all over Liverpool and Birkenhead – could not depress the gutsy Birkonians. The last bombs fell on Merseyside on 10 January 1942, and the long-suffering people could look back and say, 'That was my battle. I helped to win a victory'.

Perhaps one of the most fitting memorials of World War Two in Birkenhead was the drab ruin of the Argylle Theatre. From September 1940 until 1972, the shell of the variety theatre stood on the left of Argyll Street South, a horrid reminder of the

Slatey Road Police Station, heavily damaged after bombing raids in 1940.

terror bombing of the Blitz. Birkonians walked past and, in their heads, heard the voices of Hetty King, Ted Ray, Bud Flanagan and Chesney Allen or the songs of Florrie Forde. Now the versatile theatre of D.J. Clarke and his sons was gone. Only the Argyle Theatre pub, a driving school and a costume hiring business remained. For a generation it stood, evoking nostalgia in passers-by until the ruins were cleared away to make space for Messrs Beattie's department store car park.

During the war, and after the bombing of the Argylle Theatre, the town's entertainment was provided by the cinemas and small theatrical companies such as the Carlton Players, formed in 1930 in their Little Theatre in Grange Road West, as well as many amateur productions. Birkenhead Dramatic Society began in 1906, managed by Harold Smith, brother of F.E. Smith. The famous Birkenhead Operatic Society, founded in 1938 as a concert party to entertain troops and raise money for charities, and after the war, in 1946, it became the successful operatic society it is today. Its first fully-fledged production was *Rose Marie* in 1949.

By 1940 many of the town's theatres had become cinemas. W.W. Kelly's Theatre Royal in Argyle Street was sold to become the Savoy cinema. The Savoy was Art Deco in design, both inside and out, a glamourous evening venue where *Mrs Miniver* and *Gone With The Wind* were to raise flagging spirits in the austere 1940s. The Ritz cinema in Conway Street, another Art Deco palace, had been opened with great splendour on 4 October 1937 by the famous star Gracie Fields. This was the epitome of opulent 1930s luxury. *The Man in Possession*, starring Robert Taylor

Park Station, Birkenhead, another victim of the Blitz in March 1941.

and Jean Harlow, was shown on the first night. The Ritz was a notable new building of white Portland stone, steel and glass, with a central window tower was crowned with an illuminated cupola. Robert Cromie FRIBA (Fellow of Royal Institute of British Architects), the famed designer of many theatres, was its architect.

Sadly, on Saturday 21 December 1940, at about 9pm, just three months after the raid on the Argyll Theatre, German bombs fell on Birkenhead again and the Ritz was demolished with 100 casualties. Other cinemas in the town continued, grasping hold of the old philosophy that 'the show must go on'. The Empire, the Gaumont, the Plaza and others remained open to provide some relief for a hard-pressed public. All of these showpieces were typical of the lavish 1930s–1940s chromium-plated and plush upholstered style.

The cinemas also provided an important news service to the public. *Pathe News* bulletins spread propaganda and jingoistic, messages of patriotism, but in 1945 audiences were horrified when the first pictures of the newly-liberated concentration camps of Belsen and Auschwitz were shown. For the first time the ultimate horrors of the Nazi regime were all too evident.

The men of the Cammell Laird shipyard continued their outstanding war effort, building 106 fighting ships. A man might lose his home to a German bomb during the night but he would be at work punctually in the morning. A man might be worried about the progress of the war, heartbroken by sad news even, but at the shipyard he worked on. Many ships and submarines were launched and many were lost in battle. The *Ark Royal*, after sinking the German ship *Bismarck* in open sea off Iceland on 27 May 1941, was herself sunk off Gibraltar on 14 November 1941

by a German torpedo. *HMS Prince of Wales* had carried Winston Churchill to meet President Roosevelt in the Western Atlantic in August 1941. On 10 December 1941 the *Prince of Wales*, together with *HMS Repulse*, was attacked and sunk by Japanese aircraft torpedoes off the coast of Malaya. In all 762 lives were lost. The submarine *HMS Saracen* was sunk on 18 August 1942, torpedoed by an Italian corvette off Corsica.

The lost vessels needed replacing and many more needed repairs. Cammell Laird had an impressive wartime record for repairs to damaged ships. Some 120 warships, 9 battleships, 11 aircraft carriers and 2,000 merchant vessels all received first-aid.

The loyalty and gallantry of the people of Birkenhead and the workers of Cammell Laird was recognised when George VI and Queen Elizabeth paid special visits to the town in 1940. On 29 August they toured the shipyards, and also the districts of Birkenhead that had suffered damage from incendiaries. After the heavy raids of November, the King and Queen returned on 6 November to see for themselves and offer comfort to the victims of the Blitz. Their visits boosted morale but were overshadowed by the heaviest bombings in March 1941.

Among the heroes of Birkenhead was John Dobson, serving in the *Dalesman*. He was landed in Crete after the *Dalesman* sank in Sudla Bay, avoided capture by German paratroops and escaped with 24 others in a landing craft. He, being the only qualified navigator aboard, guided the overloaded vessel safely to Egypt, after a hazardous 10-day journey.

The end of the war in 1945 was an occasion for almost hysterical rejoicing. After

Devastation in Borough Road after the bombing of 8 May 1941. The Children's Hospital and Congregational church on Oxton Road, seen in the background, were virtually undamaged.

Bomb damage at Beer's nursery, Woodchurch Road, Birkenhead.

much anticipation 8 May 1945 was declared Victory in Europe Day. Winston Churchill announced that the Germans had signed the document of surrender, and broadcast to the nation at 3pm – 'This is your victory'. In Birkenhead there were impromptu street parties, singing, open-air dancing and parades. The heaving mass of humanity in the square was euphoric and determined to 'party until dawn'. The streets were alive with jitterbugs, congas and the hokey-kokey. But the hub of celebration was Hamilton Square, decorated with flags and bunting. The Town Hall still displayed National Savings posters and a sign above the entrance pediment, 'We want a million.'

As the evening drew on, the square became a blaze of red, white and blue light from more than 6,000 light bulbs. Over the columns of the Town Hall portico a massive symbolic 'V for Victory' glittered red white and blue. There was now no need for a blackout, instead it was fireworks and music. No command to 'put that light out'. Light starvation was over, and now there was no holding back.

The civil defence services would soon be returned to civilian duties, as would the ARP wardens, the Red Cross services, and the WRVS. Soon the Home Guard would be disbanded and the forces demobilised, but there was still work to be done. The war in the East dragged on and it seemed as if it would never end. Then, on 4 August 1945, after the absolute devastation and appalling loss of life caused by the use of two atomic bombs on Hiroshima and Nagasaki, Japan surrendered. World War Two was finally over and 11 August 1945 – VJ-Day – was a celebration riot. This time a special display of fireworks on the River Mersey set the seal on Birkenhead as a leading 'pleasure dome'. People came from all over Liverpool to see the illuminations. And again the town boogied at Hamilton Square all night long.

Work on rebuilding Britain had begun with a General Election on Thursday 5 July. Glorious weather and a very heavy turnout was a fitting climax to one of the shortest and sharpest General Election campaigns in history. Throughout Birkenhead, stations reported that 65 to 80 percent of voters went to the polls that day. Labour won Birkenhead East, Frank Soskice defeating Graham White who had held the seat as Liberal MP for 16 years. Mr Percy Collick (Labour) won Birkenhead West from Captain A.R. Moody (Conservative) in what had been a Conservative stronghold. This was a day of bitter disappointment for Graham White, who had been devoted to the welfare of Birkenhead, and an MP for 16 years. He had served as a town councillor, was chairman of Birkenhead and District Employment Committee, had served as Assistant Postmaster-General and become a privy councillor prior to 1945 election. He had served in many government departments and had been a member of Liverpool University Council. Mr White had hoped to help in the revitalisation of the town after the war but his hopes were dashed. Frank Soskice declared 'The people of Birkenhead indicated by their vote that they wish to see an active policy of reconstruction put into practice. Like the nation, Birkenhead swings left!' Clement Attlee became the new Prime Minister.

After the rejoicings of the spring and summer, Birkenhead began to prepare for

More bomb damage at the lower end of Grange Road.

Still on Grange Road, enemy bombing hit Allanson's department store.

peace and the return of her demobilised men. Homes fit for heroes was the order of the day, despite the continued shortages of food, clothes and luxuries. This need had been under review by the town council since the bombing raids of 1940 and 1941 had demolished miles of dwellings in Birkenhead. In 1944 Professor Sir Charles Reilly, an authority on town planning, had been commissioned by the Birkenhead County Borough Council to draw up a town planning scheme. The scheme was modern and ambitious, providing for the best in education and recreation for the people of Birkenhead, but improved housing was the key feature of the plan. It was recommended that 6,000 dwellings were immediately needed to replace unfit properties, houses destroyed in the bombing and to make up the shortfall of those not built during the war.

The country district and suburb of Woodchurch was planned for extensive development within Reilly's plan. Woodchurch was to retain its rural aspect in design and incorporate wide roads, village greens and airy surroundings for cottage-style dwellings. Though the scheme would be expensive, it was hailed as revolutionary and ahead of its time – in that sense an echo of the original Gillespie-Graham plan for Birkenhead of 1824. As Birkenhead had appeared, with glory, in *Illustrated London News* in 1847, Birkenhead's Woodchurch Estate was to have coverage in *Picture Post* in July 1944. However, it was rejected in favour of a scheme by Mersey Tunnel architect Herbert J. Rowse.

War damage to the hydraulic tower at Birkenhead Docks in 1940. It supplied power for dock gates and bridges. The damage was not completely repaired – the second storey south was not rebuilt and the open lantern above the tower was later removed.

*Woodchurch Post Office
c.1900.*

This scheme would have been a visual success, but this was also replaced and the whole continued by T.A. Brittain, Birkenhead's borough architect in 1952. The entire affair of the plans caused such consternation within the council, with members fighting for acceptance of one or another of the schemes, that the subsequent arguments became known as the 'Battle of the Plans'. The estate was eventually completed, though built to inferior standards of design, and opened in 1949.

The Reilly plan made many observations and suggestions which would have merit today. Firstly, Hamilton Square could be brightened up, a suggestion which was given weight by the popularity of the Victory decorations. Secondly, the illuminations could be extended to Woodside Front. A casino and a 'crystal palace' at Woodside were suggested to draw new interest and business to Birkenhead. Thirdly, the war years in particular underlined the Birkonian community spirit, when neighbour helped neighbour, especially during the Blitz. The genial cooperation of families was especially evident in providing street parties and entertainment for children and adults during the victory. This spirit should be encouraged by community planning in future.

To some extent these principles have been adopted and put into effect in the town since 1944. Other housing schemes were also adopted. The post-war Mount Estate in Prenton has 502 corporation houses set in a wooded hillside, and a further 530 houses with a shopping centre in a dell of the parish, close to the ancient Prenton

Woodchurch village at the turn of the century. Woodchurch was a rural backwater before the post-war development of Birkenhead and the building of a new housing estate in 1947.

Woodchurch village c.1908. The post office is on the right with the tower of the Church of the Holy Rood in the background.

Hall Farm of 1341. In 1949 the long-awaited Woodchurch Estate was officially opened – the culmination of the Rowse development plan and an end to the Battle of the Plans.

The previous year, on 2 February, the foundation stone of Birkenhead's new Bromborough Power Station was laid, promising improved electricity services for the town. The Labour government would soon nationalise the industry. From 1953 MANWEB supervised the power station. Although conditions and facilities in the town were now being improved, there was still a degree of social unrest. A 40-day strike of dock workers in Birkenhead came to an end on 5 November 1945. The strike, which began at the West Float in Birkenhead, reached national proportions, paralysing shipping and freezing commercial flow of the country's major industries, trade or manufacture, at all major ports. Troops were brought in to load and unload cargo. This was the longest strike action since 1911. Final agreement was reached on 25 November, when the men accepted minimum pay of 19s per day, or £5 4s 6d per week, improved working conditions and a further review of pay to a future rate of 25s per day in the near future. The action seemed to spark off similar strikes in other areas of work in the town, especially the laundry workers in conjunction with UCLA union. To quote the press at the time, this was a 'strike for better pay after years of poverty'.

The early post-war years were somewhat bleak. Shortages were actually worse than during the war, and rationing, of food, clothing and luxuries like sweets, was

'Homes fit for Heroes'. Renowned Liverpool architect Herbert J. Rowse's plan for Woodchurch Estate commenced in 1946–7.

stricter. But the people of Birkenhead still found time to celebrate. 15 January 1946 was a red-letter-day in the town, when the 60th anniversary of the Shaftesbury Boys' Club was celebrated. The club had been founded at Chester Street Mission Sunday School on 15 January 1886, for 'street boys and working lads'. William Laird Junior opened the club, which was named after the great reformer Anthony Ashley Cooper, Earl of Shaftesbury. The purpose of the club was to meet the needs of a 'large and increasing number of hungry and half-clad boys whose occupations keep them on the streets in cold and wet weather'. The club, which began as an intimate, cosy 'second home' – or first home in many instances, developed over the years into a sophisticated young men's social club with many devoted members who were to become pillars of society, and many of whom laid down their lives during the Boer War and succeeding two world wars.

A very grand event on 3 May 1950 brought flag-waving crowds to a bunting-draped Birkenhead, when Queen Elizabeth visited the town to launch the Cammell Laird-built battleship *HMS Ark Royal*. This was the first occasion that a ship built on the banks of the Mersey had been launched by a queen of England. The battleship was the second to bear the famous name built at

Coronation Villa, the 1,000th house built on the Woodchurch Estate in 1952.

Woodchurch Estate shops. The idealised cottage-style shopping centre.

137

*Pine Walks, Highpoint,
Prenton, 1947.*

Laird's, the first having been sunk in the Mediterranean in 1940. Queen Elizabeth later laid the foundation stone of the Birkenhead Technical College. The very nature of Birkenhead, and its industry, demanded technical education in the town. The town had been, and always would be, built on its industry, especially on the skills associated with shipbuilding.

William Jackson had incorporated such education in his Albert Memorial Industrial School. John Laird carried the idea further in giving his Laird School of Art to the town. Birkenhead Institute offered, in its first prospectus in 1889, provision for technical education of the best kind.

For 50 years from 1877, the centre for technical education had been Holt Technical School. Adult education and private commercial education was provided at Beechcroft, an old house at the bottom of Whetstone Lane in the centre of town.

Between 1914 and 1924, Cecile and Horace Fleming had established the Beechcroft Educational Settlement, which had grown out of the Oxton Road Adult School in 1905. The school blended Workers' Education Authority service, church service and Liverpool University tutorial classes for the working man and woman. H. Graham White, MP for Birkenhead, was much involved during the Depression, when the settlement sought to alleviate Birkenhead's problems of unemployment and bad housing, and provide purposeful academic education for men and women out of work. There was even a nursery for women with children. In 1924, from being an educational settlement funded by voluntary contributions, Beechcroft was

Allanson's stores, 1947. Purchased by Beattie's of Wolverhampton in the 1970s.

Allanson's as it looked when founded in 1860.

A suggestion for the Outline Plan of Birkenhead, by Professor Sir Charles Reilly in 1947. Drawn by Peter Shepheard in 1944, Woodside Ferry Casino was never realised.

eventually taken over by the Local Education Authority and continued a valuable WEA service. The Birkenhead Technical College was to provide adult education services after 1955.

Plans for a specific technical education college were prepared in the later years of the 1930s. The war intervened, and the project was not carried out until 1950. It was completed in 1955 and opened, with ceremony, by Lord Cohen of Birkenhead, an old boy of Birkenhead Institute.

Coronation year, 1953, marked the beginning of what was called a new 'Elizabethan Age'. The year was also marked with an honour for the Birkenhead Constabulary when Sir David Maxwell Fyfe, Secretary of State for the Home Department, opened the new police headquarters near Hamilton Square on 30 October. For the police service that had begun as three night watchmen and a parish constable in 1837 it marked the arrival of a modern police force which had welcomed its first female officers during World War One. In the intervening years the force had survived the disastrous police strike of 1919, the stressful Blitz of the 1940s and the bombing of Price Street police station on 13 March 1941. The force now consisted of 410 officers, and the improved HQ contained every technological assistance and equipment then available. A special section to deal with serious crime, a dog-handling section, an attendance centre for youthful offenders and a juvenile liaison scheme were all added to the service. In 1967 the Birkenhead police force was to stand down and become the Birkenhead Division of Cheshire Constabulary.

The fire service had been a section of the police force since 1843, when local interested insurance companies provided a fire engine for the force at a cost of £200, as a means of keeping claims at bay. A breakaway fire service was appointed in the

1880s and a new and impressive purpose-built headquarters was built in Whetstone Lane. In 1972 the HQ became too small to allow efficient service and an even larger complex, providing 24-hour operational service, was opened in Exmouth Street in March the following year.

In 1957, the new Queen of five years paid a visit to Birkenhead, on Thursday 11 July, arriving at 3.20pm in teeming rain. This was Elizabeth II at her most youthful – serene in a steel blue sculptured taffeta coat and whisp-pink petalled hat. Shadowed by her striking husband, HRH the Duke of Edinburgh, she charmed the enormous mass standing drenched in Hamilton Square. The brief, glamourous occasion was in no way diminished by the dreary weather. Elizabeth wowed the crowds.

This was also the day on which Birkenhead's favourite regiment, 4th Battalion Cheshires, were presented

Another Shepheard drawing of the same year for the Outline Plan, this time for a new Woodside Hotel.

Birkenhead Technical College entrance hall. Typical Festival of Britain era decor, by Willink and Dodd, 1950–4.

Traffic congestion at the Mersey Tunnel entrance at peak periods, such as this in 1955, led eventually to a new road system incorporating flyovers. It was inaugurated by Barbara Castle in March 1967.

with new colours by the Queen on the Roodee at Chester, just 48 years after their last presentation by Edward VII. All in all it was a day to remember.

The Queen arrived in Birkenhead just a few months after the 100th anniversary of the Birkenhead library service, on 3 December 1956. In that year it was recorded that some 15,000 volumes would be in the hands of adult readers every day, and children held 3,000 books daily. The library service had grown from a simple fire-lit room in Price Street, to a monolithic Central Library on Borough Road and five large branch libraries throughout the town. Over the years clever academics had been appointed librarians in charge, from Richard Hinton, John Shepherd and George Stratton to Herbert (Harry) H.G. Arthur and, latterly, J. Ian Coles. Each of these gentlemen brought his personal skills to bear in the administration of the service. Richard Hinton was founder librarian and established a fine collection of books, some of which remain a nucleus of the valuable antiquarian collection. John Shepherd nurtured the new, modern service, which opened in 1934 with the building of the new Central Library and established the library's reputation for excellent librarianship. George Stratton saw the service through the days of World War Two and broadened the provision of services, including extramural services, the Williamson Art Gallery and the Allied Museum Service in the post-war period. Harry Arthur was aware of the modern expansion of technology in providing information and library services. He introduced new equipment and methods of research to that end. Ian Coles created a body of efficient librarians and assistants on the new lines of management within local government appropriate to the late 1980s and up to date. The great IT revolution, and especially the advent of the world wide web, is transporting today's Birkenhead library user and researcher to the virtual galaxies. Birkenhead's modern librarian is computer literate and internet articulate.

The Ritz cinema in Conway Street, bombed in 1940, had been restored, renovated and reopened in January 1947. The opening was a gala at which the band of the 22nd Cheshire Regiment performed, famous soprano Gwen Catley sang, and Lionel Gamlin presented some of the programme. The chosen film was *Blue Skies* with Fred Astaire and Bing Crosby. After this, manager Bill Boht (former husband of local actress Jean Boht) was to arrange regular programmes with special guests including some of the most famous personalities of the day like

Birkenhead Technical College, the mural decorating the entrance hall depicts Wirral history, photographed c.1955. Sadly later removed and lost, it would have been a visual epitome of this history.

Bebe Daniels, Ben Lyon, Valerie Hobson, Gregory Peck, Leslie Hutchinson, Wilson, Keppel and Betty to add to famous films such as *The Forsyte Saga*.

The Ritz, with its famous restaurant managed by Reece's Catering, was the favourite rendezvous for post-war Wirralians after a day's shopping in Grange Road, Grange Road West and Birkenhead market. Audience figures began to fall in the late 1950s and, after a disastrous takeover by Essoldo Cinemas in the 1960s, the Ritz finally closed on Sunday 5 January 1969. It was not a good time for the old picture palaces. The 1960s saw the gradual fading of the cinema, attributable to the popularity of television – for the first time available in most homes. Many of the cinemas, unable to compete and survive, were being transformed into the ever-popular bingo hall.

1967 saw the opening of the Woodchurch Community Centre by Alderman Hugh Platt. The complex included swimming baths, a sports hall, theatre, youth club and welfare offices all designed to provide leisure interests for the residents of the Woodchurch Estate.

The visit of darling of the Labour Party, Barbara Castle, the Transport Minister to officially inaugurated Birkenhead's tunnel approach road improvement scheme on 17 March 1967 marked a significant change in the town. 'Traffic thrombosis' was Birkenhead's abiding ailment, with the increased use of the motor car and the popularity of tunnel access to Liverpool. Two years later, on 15 July 1969, Robin S.Colquhoun, project engineer, saw his multi-million-pound tunnel motorway and fly-over opened by Alderman Hugh Platt, leader of Birkenhead town council.

The technical college, Borough Road. Now a department of Wirral Metropolitan College, the building was opened by Sir Henry Cohen. Queen Elizabeth laid the foundation stone in 1950. The lecture hall and, later, Glenda Jackson Theatre is far right foreground. Soon to be demolished, 2003.

The late 1960s were a time of great social improvements. Lord Cohen of Birkenhead opened the Social Services Centre in Cleveland in 1967. The £370,000 building would be a nerve centre for health services and the promotion of the borough's good health. Lord Cohen then crossed the street to the newly-built multi-storey municipal office block, where a commemorative plaque was unveiled by Alderman Jack Oates. The building, costing £594,000, was the tallest in Hamilton Square, with a sky-high canteen, golden, solar-reflective windows and golden mosaic-covered walls. Known as the Orange Building, the treasury building was to suffer a sad fate.

'Skyscrapers' were in fashion in Birkenhead and, in an effort to use space economically, on 21 April 1958, Birkenhead MP Percy Collick (Labour) had opened the town's first multi-storey flats in two buildings at the north end. Oak and Eldon Gardens were sadly to become notorious, unsociable residences where many tearaways lived, and suffer another sad fate. The flats had promised every modern convenience – even underfloor heating – in a clean and airy location. They were the first buildings in the country to be constructed by the new method of building. However, the tenants were to find themselves isolated, lonely and deserted at the top of endless stairs when lifts failed or were damaged. There were no facilities for children's play, and consequently some mothers, especially, suffered depression and allied mental problems.

Children and youths with idle hands had always been present in Birkenhead. Charles Thompson's Mission, the Newsboys' Club, industrial schools and the Shaftesbury Boys' Club were all active in meeting the need to occupy the youth of the town. The YMCA played a great part and, in the 1960s and 1970s, became

Congestion at Mersey Tunnel Birkenhead entrance on Market Place South, 1960s.

important in projecting the Duke of Edinburgh's Award Scheme which he had founded in 1956. Royal patronage was not wanting. The Duchess of Kent visited the YMCA building in Whetstone Lane and sampled the courses and activities designed to make young Birkonians fit, active and alert members of the town. In 1972 HRH Prince Philip visited the centre to see some of the work done for the Duke of Edinburgh Award Scheme. He met the wardens, Mr and Mrs Stanley Griffiths, and young people and helpers at the association.

Sport in the town had a special role in occupying young people and adults alike. The local authority set great store by its provision of sports and leisure facilities in building character and good citizenship in the people of Birkenhead. Swimming baths and leisure centres were well attended in the 1960s and 1970s. Byrne Avenue baths had the famed Birkenhead Swimming Club, Woodchurch Community Centre featured a handicapped swimming club and the leisure centre in Grange Road West was well-equipped for indoor sports.

The spectacular lawns and open spaces of Birkenhead Park created in 1847, when the ladies and gentlemen of the upper classes sought healthful recreation, could only provide the perfect venue. And so the Park Cricket Club was founded in 1846–7. One, clearly none too serious, match of 1847 involved 77 players! In 1864 Lancashire County Cricket Club played against Park in two matches. Two years later an all-England side lost four matches of six they played against Park. Cecil Holden was one of the best cricketers to turn out for Birkenhead's oldest cricket

Birkenhead Central Library, children's library, showing Miss Garlick, library assistant, 1950s.

club. He scored 202 against 'Northern' in a match in 1896. The bat he used was later presented to the club by Mr Frank Edwards. The Park 1st XI of 1931 tied with Wallasey CC for the championship of their league due mainly to Park's new professional fast bowler Jack Bartley, whose haul was 67 wickets at an average of 10.37 over 26 matches.

Another professional was 'Mad Jack' Jackson – a nickname derived from his odd postures and comic antics – a leading fast bowler in England and coach at Birkenhead School between 1878 and 1880.

Birkenhead Park Rugby Club was formed in 1871. Park have been playing in the Upper Park, Birkenhead from 1886 and every season since. James 'Bim' Baxter, who played for England and was later President of the English Selection Committee, began playing with Park in 1889, and only his death in 1943 ended his association with the club. Baxter was one of Park's greatest celebrities and one of the guiding figures in rugby football. He was largely responsible for England's rugby successes between the wars. Two other Park stars were Harold Locke and Wilfred Lowry. They scored 15 tries between them when the Park side beat Sale 65-0 in 1924. The club survives to this day and still provides plenty of entertainment as well as breeding plenty of fine rugby players for internationals and county matches in Cheshire and her neighbouring counties.

Since 1881, excitement for so many Birkonians has meant Tranmere Rovers Football Club, which was formed in that year under the presidency of Alderman James H. McGaul, Conservative councillor for Clifton Ward. Beginning as a club

Leyland Titan PD2/40 No.49 at Woodside. This view demonstrates the immaculate appearance of Birkenhead Transport vehicles during the early 1960s. Birkenhead bus services were run by Mr Bob Cherry. They were regarded as the best in the country – never late, frequent, clean, efficient and reasonably-priced. They never failed throughout the Blitz and right up to the 1970s. Blue and Cream, Pride of the Wirral.

Birkenhead Park Rugby Union club centenary game.

playing friendly matches, by 1887 Rovers had acquired 1,000 supporters, was charging admission and playing on Prenton Park.

Rovers prospered and in 1907–8 won their first championship and Combination Cup. In 1921 they were admitted to the Football League's new Third Division North. They were promoted to Division Two in the 1937–8 season, but finished bottom of the table and were relegated. However, before they could try again, League football was closed down following the outbreak of World War Two.

In August 1946, Rovers resumed in the Third Division North but enjoyed no further success until they finished in the top half in 1957–8 to form the new Third Division, the lower clubs in each section forming the Fourth, to where Rovers themselves were relegated in 1960–1. For the next few years Rovers went between the two divisions and in December 1968, Dennis Howell, Minister for Sport and a former Football League referee, opened the club's new 4,000-seater stand. In 1972, a crowd of 24,424 saw the FA Cup game against Stoke City. This was the club's record attendance. The club went into decline and was almost extinguished when Bruce Ostermann from the USA took control. His enthusiasm for football outmatched his business skills, and he ran up debts of over £500,000. In 1987 local millionaire Peter Johnson rescued the club from ruin when he took control. New barriers and fences were installed with floodlights costing £70,000

In 1991 when they returned to the Second Division via the play-offs. That division was renamed the First with the advent of the Premier League and for three years in succession Rovers themselves toyed with promotion to the top flight of English football but never got past the first round of the play-offs. By 1993 Tranmere Rovers had risen from Fourth to Second Division, but their financial

The Argyle Theatre, early 1970s, just prior to demolition.

fortunes waned in 1994 due to huge costs (£3.1 million) in building work to complete improved safety measures at the ground. In 2001 Rovers went back to what was now the new Second Division. A year earlier Rovers supporters had travelled to Wembley in their thousands when their club reached the Worthington Cup Final, where they lost to Leicester City.

In 2003 fans look to a hopeful future with Ray Mathias as the manager. His slogan is 'We battle on'.

Over the years, Tranmere Rovers have fielded some of the greatest players in the game. Legendary goalscorer Dixie Dean was born in Birkenhead, signed for Rovers in January 1924 and the following season scored 27 goals in 27 games before, in March 1925, moving to Goodison Park for £3,000. For Everton he set a league record – which still stands – of 60 goals in one season, 1927–8.

Birkenhead-born Bunny Bell scored a triple hat-trick in the Football League with nine goals against Oldham Athletic in 1935. Altogether Bunny – whose real name was Robert Charles – had the remarkable strike rate of 102 goals in only 114 League games for Tranmere Rovers before moving to Everton in 1935.

Pongo Waring, yet another native of Birkenhead, signed as a professional for Rovers in January 1926 and early in 1928 hit six of the eleven goals which Tranmere scored against Durham City. This came in a spell in which he scored 24 goals in 27 games. Waring moved to Aston Villa in 1928, for £4,700, and in one season alone, 1930–1, scored 50 goals for them. As a youth, it was reported that his teammates said he had 'fragrant' feet.

For centre-half Harold Bell, Tranmere Rovers was his only club, but he appeared for them no less than 595 times during the 1940s and 1950s. Staggeringly, between 1946 and 1954, Bell played in 401 consecutive League games to establish another record which stands today and is now unlikely ever to be beaten.

Roy McFarland was transferred from Rovers to Derby County in August 1967, for £25,000, after the Derby manager Brian Clough got him out of bed in the small hours of the morning to sign. McFarland shared in all Derby's success under Clough and was also England's regular centre-half.

In 2003, 19-year-old Ian Hance was a player of promise, while his team-mate Simon Howarth proved a quicksilver forward. Although in the perpetual shadow of Premiership giants Liverpool and Everton, Tranmere Rovers keep their side of the Mersey bubbling on match days as the fans still flock to Prenton Park.

The decorative stone sign board, exterior wall of the theatre, dating from 1868. removed to Williamson Art Gallery in 1973 before demolition.

Although almost unnoticed by the townspeople, 1974 was a year of great change in Birkenhead and in the country. This was the realisation of local government reorganisation, when five local authorities in Wirral were fused into the Metropolitan Borough of Wirral. This new monster devoured the County Borough of Birkenhead, her town hall and her fine council chamber. However, her golden building continued as the hub of financial power in the new borough, a key and powerful new-age technical control centre for the new authority. It is significant that the last mayor of Birkenhead should be Alderman Miss Eileen M. Keegan, last of a number of notable female mayors, Mrs Mary Anne Mercer having been the first to hold that honour in 1924. As Miss Keegan said in 1974, 'We must all now go forward into the new community full of hope.'

Bidston windmill 1974, sails anchored. Now much restored and open to the public on the first Sunday of each month.

Part 7

THE RACE TO IMPROVE THE TOWN AND RAISE ITS PROFILE FROM 1974 TO DATE

T HE County Borough of Birkenhead ceased to exist on 1 April 1974, when the sound of footsteps heralded the movement of local government officers from old occupations to new locations throughout the newly-created Metropolitan Borough of Wirral.

By faith and foresight', five districts of the peninsula were fused into one. Birkenhead, Wallasey, Bebington, Heswall and Hoylake were united. Birkenhead remained the leading town, bringing a wealth of services and talent to the new Metropolitan Borough, including her town clerk Ian Holt, who was appointed chief executive. Mr Holt had been deputy town clerk in Wallasey from 1959–62 and then moved to the position of town clerk of Birkenhead.

Mr Holt's interests in sport and music, and his particularly keen support of Tranmere Rovers FC, were reflected in his life and work in the town. He was to retire in 1983 after a stormy career as chief executive of the council, during which many heated arguments took place in the council chamber. He died in autumn 1996.

The ancient ferry service at Woodside and the hallowed ruins of the Priory remained the historic foundation of the Merseyside settlement despite all the changes which had taken place over the centuries. 1974 saw the abiding problem of striking industrial manpower take ruinous hold on Birkenhead.

Year on year, many Birkenhead people had suffered social deprivation which required social reform and assistance. The party that promised to provide that reform was the Labour Party, and so, after the General Election of 1945, Labour candidates were routinely elected to Parliament and to the council in Birkenhead. The trades union movement had already become influential in favour of the labour force of the town during the slumps and hardships of the 1920s and 1930s. Percy Collick, MP for Birkenhead West from 1945 to 1964, was also assistant general secretary of ASLEF (Associated Society of Locomotive Engineers and Firemen).

Hillbark, Frankby. Formerly Bidston Court, built in Bidston for MacGregor Laird, and moved stone-by-stone to its present site 1929–31.

Labour's Edmund Dell succeeded Percy Collick in 1964. He served as Trade Secretary under James Callaghan and was Paymaster General in Harold Wilson's 1974 government. He left politics in 1979 for a troublesome career in banking. The electorate of Birkenhead criticised Dell for the scandalous unemployment in the town in 1978.

After the General Election of 1979 Dell's place was taken by Birkenhead's present Labour MP Frank Field. At 36, Frank Field was director of Child Poverty Action Group, a truly appropriate qualification for a Birkenhead MP. In 1979 he said, 'Birkenhead has 8,000 unemployed. The total bill of all their costs in supplements etc, also the lost wealth because people are not working, comes to something like £78 million a year, but we prefer to keep people idle.' Frank Field has been the champion of children, women, the elderly, the unemployed, the sick and all those unaware of their rights – especially to benefits – from the time of his election to Parliament. As Minister for Welfare Reform in 1998, he introduced the Welfare to Work Initiative to help young jobless under the New Deal. His influence was short-lived due to Tony Blair's reshuffle of the Cabinet in 1998, when Frank Field resigned his post and returned to the back benches.

The shipbuilding industry, which had been the foundation of Birkenhead's growth and hoped-for prosperity in 1820, was at a new turn of fortune in 1974. The huge labour force in Birkenhead and the wealth of the town depended, once again, on the success of Laird's.

Demolition of Oak and Eldon Gardens, Birkenhead, by explosives, 30 September 1979. Eldon Gardens crash to the ground from the charges.

The final stage, the last of Eldon Gardens falls after some delay.

Although merchant ships, warships and submarines had been built at Laird's in the 1950s and 1960s – to whit the missile destroyer *HMS Devonshire*, 1962; the frigate *HMS Ajax*, 1963; three Oberon Class submarines, 1963; *British Ensign* oil tanker for BP – 1963 and 1964 proved poor years for the yard. A strike of the shipwrights lasted three months, and their pay claim was unsuccessful. This capitulation saw a turnaround in attitude, organised labour becoming more determined from that point.

The British Government's Polaris project and nuclear submarine-building began in 1967. These new projects required changes in management, work standards and in the workforce – three factors that resulted in resentments, strike actions and the eventual failure of the company. Robert White Johnson, managing director, said 'Once people know that they're going to be paid in any case, your bargaining position is undermined and the workforce is more prone to strike, and the management yield to the pressure.'

Sovereign Explorer *The 'Pride of Merseyside'. The first oil-rig to be built on Merseyside at Cammell Laird's shipyard. Launched for Dome Petroleum on 6 December 1983.*

A closer look at Sovereign Explorer.

In 1967 M.J. Wyatt, director, sent a message to the workforce: 'There is clear evidence that some workers are not pulling their weight... they defraud the company and themselves of higher wages.' New managers – considered by some to be nothing more than nuclear technocrats – were brought in. A workforce of 8,280 in 1960 increased to 11,400 in 1969. The *HMS Renown* nuclear submarine was launched on 25 February 1967 by Mrs Edna Healey, wife of the Minister of Defence Denis Healey. There followed *HMS Revenge* and *HMS Conqueror*, and, launched in 1972, the Polaris-capable submarine, one of which – *HMS Conqueror*, sank the Argentinian ship *General Belgrano* during the Falklands conflict in 1982.

These vessels were the last big job that Cammell Laird completed before the crash of 1970. The nuclear submarine-building programme was to be continued, without competitive tender, at Vickers' yard in Barrow-in-Furness. Many Cammell Laird men were made redundant, and the workforce reduced. Some important ships were still being built, as well as the oil platform *Sovereign Explorer*, 1983, but upgrading of the yard in 1972 came too late and the company was eventually nationalised as part of British Shipbuilders. This helped little though, since throughout the 1970s there were innumerable trades and workforce disputes which resulted in downed tools and stoppages, all to the further detriment of the company. Orders dwindled and Cammell Laird was then denationalised. The yard became a subsidiary of VSEL of Barrow in 1985 but the yard never really recovered. The last vessel built at Laird's, and launched in April 1992, was the submarine *HMS Unicorn*.

Pyramids Shopping Precinct from Borough Road, Birkenhead, September 1989.

Cammell Laird closed down for the last time on 31 July 1993. The walls, and some of the buildings, remain on Chester Road. The archive of documents and photographs is housed at Wirral Museum in Birkenhead Town Hall.

Pyramids with new traffic layout, September 1989.

Though the economic situation seemed gloomy, the 1970s saw the introduction of a number of improvements in the cultural life of the town. After 1974 the Birkenhead Arts Association began an energetic programme of cultural events to promote performing arts, theatre, cinema and concert in the town, much as the arts enthusiasts of Edwardian Birkenhead had done. One popular annual event was an open-air performance of a work by Shakespeare, promoted and advertised by Birkenhead Arts, but staged by Hillbark Players of Frankby. The first performance, in May 1976, was in the grounds of Hillbark, a fine pseudo-Elizabethan half-timbered mansion, built in 1891 for MacGregor Laird, shipbuilder, by the architect Edward Ould. At that time the house was named Bidston Court. It stood in Vyner Road South, Bidston. In 1929, Robert Hudson, soap manufacturer, bought Bidston Court and had it transported brick-by-brick to Royden Park in Frankby. Recreated, the house was renamed Hillbark. It was used for many of the open-air Shakespearian plays until 1992.

Birkenhead Library Film Society was founded in 1972, organised by the senior librarians,and catered for the less mainstream movie-goer. At first, films were shown at the Williamson Art Gallery. Membership was slow in building, but now the society is very popular and has been upgraded. Meetings are held in the Birkenhead Town Hall, and many recent films are shown, such as *Gosford Park*.

Birkenhead's centres of entertainment have dwindled since the heydays of the 1940s, 1950s and 1960s. Now there is no Argyle Theatre, no Theatre Royal and no Ritz cinema. The Glenda Jackson Theatre, named and opened by the locally-born

Birkenhead Park rugby club, October 1989.

TV star, actress and Labour politician in September 1982, enjoyed only a short popularity. Originally built as a wing of Birkenhead Technical College for associated academic presentations, lectures and events, in 1982 the building was assigned to public theatrical productions in an attempt to raise or supplement funds for the college. The theatre had a very short life.

In Grange Road West the Little Theatre, a converted church and home of the resident Carleton Players, still provides good entertainment throughout the year with plays, pantomimes and revues.

Many famous names have visited Birkenhead and given great performances: Valerie Masterton, Patricia Routledge, Paco Peña, Ravi Shankar, Pascal Roget, Ralph Reader and his Gang Show (fitting tribute to one of the cradles of the Scout movement) and the International Jazz Guitar Festival. The arts revival in Birkenhead reawakened interest in Birkenhead's largest concert hall, the Birkenhead Town Hall Assembly Rooms, and brought about a new determination on Wirral Borough Council's part to give the building a practical use and purpose. It became an arts venue and the centrepiece of Wirral Museums and Archives Service in 2001.

The General Hospital, the Children's Hospital and all allied town services were replaced by the wonder of the 1980s, Arrowe Park Hospital, which has 1,279 beds and whose A & E department sees 90,000 patients a year. The hospital was opened to great celebration in May 1982 by Elizabeth II. Wirral Hospital NHS Trust now controls all healthcare provision in the town.

Fourteen years later, and as a grand overture to the ongoing initiative that brought European aid to Birkenhead, the Queen and Duke of Edinburgh inaugurated the grand Europa Park complex, comprising an international business management centre, a high-tech college of education for all local students, a modern leisure complex with Olympic-standard swimming pool and modern sports facilities, a multi-screen cinema complex, a state-of-the-art bus terminal and a bright new railway station link to the Wirral Railway through to Liverpool.

J.HARE

Woodside landing stage from the new business park, June 1991.

This was the first stage in creating a broad coverage for renewed business and trading facilities, using Birkenhead as the hub of the EuroWirral expanding markets. Would William Laird have approved? Without doubt, Laird, Jackson and Brassey would have been in at the very beginning to take advantage of every business opportunity.

Some of the men's legacy has since disappeared. The Birkenhead market of 1845 – Fox, Henderson & Co's classical hall – had burned down in 1976. It was replaced by the new Market building on the Grange Road shopping precinct.

That shopping precinct, opened in 1975, replaced the busy Victorian Grange Road, and was extended outward and upward with a multi-storey car park and pedestrianised shopping malls, to become The Pyramids. Egyptian in style and decor, exotic in flavour to match the Egyptian style of Birkenhead's Art Deco tunnel building. This complex is designed to draw the customers to Birkenhead, where they may take advantage of Marks and Spencers, Beatties of Birkenhead and Wolverhampton, William Pike High Class Jewellers, Next, WH Smith, Waterstone's and Boots the Chemist. Sadly, Robb Brothers, Rostances, Tutty's, Ellison's paints and wallpapers, Irwin's the grocers, Woodside Garage, Mackenzie's electrical goods, and Watson's have all now left the town. As family businesses, they had outgrown the area of market and were replaced by newer, larger business organisations, although some of these have trickled into the hinterland of Wirral, e.g. Asda and Tesco. In 1978–9 Birkenhead was described as the heart of Wirral, but a heart that was failing. To strengthen and revitalise Birkenhead, City Lands – a five-year project – was established by Wirral Investment Network. WIN is a fusion of the Wirral Council with multinational and home-grown businesses to create prosperity for the town in much the same manner as the early 19th-century entrepreneurs of

Grange Road, August 1991.

Birkenhead. The early developments included Conway Park rail and bus station, the IBM Tech College Centre, Europa Pool and Leisure Complex and a new housing development on Conway Street. These were initiatives which have swept away the poor and shabby properties which formerly filled the north end of Birkenhead.

EuroWirral was able to take advantage of European Union grants and funding for underprivileged communities to extend the initiatives which were put into effect, such as City Lands, which operated for five years with great success.

There followed CEWTEC (Chester, Ellesmere Port and Wirral Technical Enterprise Council) which was to assist in finding local employment for local jobless and local employees for local business. It proved a successful and appropriate matching of the workforce.

Since 2001 CEWTEC has been replaced by Scientian, a new initiative which provides appropriate training and work for those seeking employment within Birkenhead.

Encouraged by government policy to foster tourism and heritage, and taking advantage of European funding, Birkenhead has been able to harness her vast historical resources to the tourist industry. The City Lands initiative provided for the building of a heritage trail through the former depressed and faded docklands of Birkenhead. Riverside walks now replace dreary quays. An historic tram service links the former ancient street railway of George Francis Train with Birkenhead's original train service.

A replica Victorian street, the elegant 19th century Hamilton Square and residential garden, the Birkenhead Town Hall, now converted to Wirral Museum and Archive, all contribute to the intriguing Birkenhead Heritage Experience. The very ancient Priory ruins and Victorian remnant, St Mary's Parish Church, plus the Cammell Laird dock site add further to this tourist attraction.

The second of Birkenhead's regeneration schemes ran for seven years. The Hamilton Quarter began in 1995. Its brief to build on Birkenhead's glorious past carried City Lands a stage further, in building business, arts and the environment as the pivot of the town. Original Victorian shopping malls in the neighbourhood of Hamilton Square, Waterloo Buildings, Market Street, Bridge Street and the Antiques Triangle, the purpose-built high-class department stores and shops designed by Gillespie Graham in the 1840s for the gentry of new Birkenhead, have now been restored and renovated. They are all converted to residential luxury apartments. The

What's cooking – the centre of the Pyramids, August 1991.

Dock gates, Woodside, August 1991.

Woodside landing stage, August 1991.

adjacent waterfront over the Mersey is now a stroll way of the heritage trail, since all sub-standard old buildings have been demolished and the famous Woodside Ferry approaches have been smartened and upgraded. On Pacific Road, once a centre of dockside industry with all the grime and bustle that implies, is now an award-winning arts and exhibition centre. The centre opened in February 1999, and is funded jointly by a European Objective One programme and the Single Regeneration Budget.

The Egerton Dock – a wonder of engineering, opened in 1847, designed by Rendel and carried to completion by Jesse Hartley – has now become a 'visitor experience'. No longer a busy port-side dock, visitors may look and learn about the history of this famous project. A model of the *Resurgam*, first submarine built in

Tower at Great Float and the redeveloped road, August 1991.

Birkenhead by J. Cochrane over 100 years ago, is displayed on the Woodside Ferry Approach as a permanent heritage attraction.

Inside the Pyramids, August 1991.

Maritime interests are further catered for at the East Float, Dock Road. Here a collection of four famous vessels is open to public view. They are minesweeper *HMS Bronington*, once under the command of HRH the Prince of Wales and officially presented to the town at a ceremony attended by the prince in 2003, *HMS Onyx* – a nuclear sub which served in the Falklands campaign, the U-boat *U534*, a German submarine, and the destroyer *HMS Plymouth*.

Since the closure of Cammell Laird's shipyard, the yards and the community of the dockside in north Birkenhead have deteriorated. A further regeneration budget was obtained – £40 million plus an original £18 million – to revive the yards and to develop an urban village for the good of 25,000 residents. The creation of Lairdside began in 1997 and was completed in 2003, having successfully revived property and improved the environment, as well as putting many young people into useful employment.

One of Birkenhead's oldest and, perhaps 'intriguing', buildings is Tam O'Shanter's cottage, which has become a favourite tourist attraction in a quaint rural setting on Bidston Hill. The cottage is dated *c.*1670 and its most famous resident was Richard Lea, a stonemason who lived there in 1837. He may well have been a Scotsman, for he carved a tablet which showed the drunken Tam O'Shanter (from the poem by Robbie Burns) on his mare Meg, escaping over a bridge from the vengeful witches, after he had been caught watching one particularly comely witch who danced in a revealing 'cutty sark' or short chemise. In 1976 the cottage was vandalised but was restored and developed as an urban farm and field study centre, and reopened in May 1977. The centre, a favourite with young and old, is of great recreational and educational value.

Woodside Business Centre, CEWTEC headquarters, October 1991.

Hamilton Square gardens, October 1991.

At least as unusual, and somewhat more quirky, is the story of the Ford Estate. This estate of 2,057 houses cloaked Ford Hill on the edge of Upton with up-to-date modern dwellings in a rural setting. Over the years, from the completion of building in 1973, an apparent curse fell over the development and the properties deteriorated. Thus, in an amazing effort and surprising strategy on the part of the local authority, a decision was taken to frustrate the stigma by turning all the houses around and making their back doors their front doors. Likewise, their gardens, outhouses, shopping areas and official centres were reversed. The properties were all renovated and, as a final change, the community was renamed the Beechwood Estate in 1994.

On 30 September 1979 two notorious tower blocks of flats were demolished. Oak and Eldon Gardens, when opened to tenants in the 1950s, had been hailed as a miracle of construction. Every flat was a luxury of modern living. However depression, drug addiction, isolation, damaged property, theft and squalor eventually proved to be the legacy of

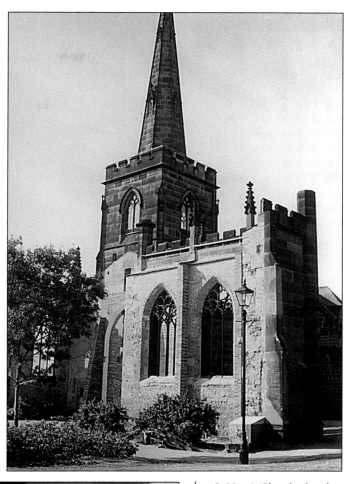

St Mary's Church after the renovation as part of the Woodside Trail, 1991. The body of the church is demolished but the tower and spire retained. One can climb 200 steps for a panoramic view of the Wirral.

The Mayor of Wirral, Mrs Myrra Lea, introduces the Queen to Wirral Metropolitan College principle Jenny Shackleton before touring and opening the new building. The opening ceremony for the Wirral International Business and Management Centre at Europa Park was performed on 7 June 1996.

Birkenhead Priory dockland development October 1991.

many of those who were forced to live there, until Red Adair and his disposal team, under the aegis of Ogden's contractors, blew up the buildings. The spectacular event drew huge crowds and was to hit the headlines. Renewal of Birkenhead had begun and much continues to be done to improve living and working conditions, leisure and culture in Birkenhead today.

Educational opportunities in the town are also benefiting from modern

The boat house, Birkenhead Park, November 1991.

MY SUBJECT IS WAR
AND THE PITY OF WAR

developments. The new Birkenhead Sixth Form College is designed to produce responsible, self-sufficient students.

With strong links to the European Union, Birkonians are now sophisticated cosmopolitans. The distant days of hooded monks, tolling vespers, hearty serfs and pilgrims' shells are gone. Here come the 21st-century Birkonians.

Perhaps one may say again, as the poet said in 1847,

'Another glory on the Mersey's side:

A town springs up as from a magic wand.' ...(Anonymous)

Mayoral coat of arms.

The Wilfred Owen Window at Birkenhead Central Library. Installed in 1995 to commemorate World War One poet Owen (1893–1918), who lived in Birkenhead from 1897–1907.

Part of the Birkenhead Heritage Trail – The 'Historic Warships' in May 2003 at Cornware House quay, East Float, Wallasey. HMS Plymouth (frigate) and HMS Onyx (submarine).

Ritz Cinema, Conway Street, opened by Gracie Fields in 1937. Refurbished after war damage the cinema reopened in 1947. This picture shows the film Penny Princess was featuring, dating it from 1953. The Ritz closed in 1969 and was demolished between 2000 and 2002.

BIBLIOGRAPHY

Albert Memorial Schools Annual Reports 1864–1903.

Aspinall, Henry Kelsall *Birkenhead and its surroundings*, 1903

Arrowe Park, Pamphlet, 1929.

Bu'lock, J.D. *Pre-Conquest Cheshire 383–1066*, 1972.

Burdett, P.P. *Map of Cheshire*, 1797.

Bidston, Carol E. *Birkenhead in times past*.

Birkenhead News, 1880 to date.

Boumphrey, Ian *Birkenhead. A Pictorial History*.

Broadbent, R.J. *Annals of the Liverpool stage*, 1908.

Cammell Laird *Shipbuilders Builders of Great Ships*.

County Borough of Birkenhead *Birkenhead 1877–1974*, 1974.

County Borough of Birkenhead *Official Guides*

Daily Arrowe (Jamboree Newspaper), various issues 1929.

Della Robbia Notes and documents held in Birkenhead Library.

Dictionary of National Biography.

Dodgson, J. McN *The Place-names of Cheshire, Part II. The Place-names of Broxton Hundred and Wirral Hundred*, 1972.

Duckworth, Christian Leslie Dyce and Graham Easton Langmuir *West Coast Streamers, 3rd ed.*, 1966.

Ellison, Norman *Wirral Peninsula*.

Encyclopaedia Britannica.

Fay, B. Essington *Life of Charles Thompson*, 1904.

Fleming, Horace *History of Beechcroft*, 1938.

Gore Liverpool directories, 1840–1976.

Hayes, Dean *Tranmere Rovers Football Club: The Complete A–Z*, 1999.

Helps, Arthur *Life and Labours of Mr Brassey, 1805–70*, 1872.

Hillhouse, David *Della Robbia Pottery, Birkenhead 1894–1906*.

Historic Society of Lancashire and Cheshire Transactions, various.

Johnson, Alan and Kevin Moore *Lees Tapestry Works*, 1987.

Law *Map of Birkenhead*, 1844.

Lee, Arthur *Arthur H. Lee and Sons Master Weaver*.

Liverpool Daily Post *Bombers over Merseyside,*, 1941.

Liverpool Mercury *Life of Sir William Jackson*, June 1876.

McIntyre, W.R.S. *Birkenhead yesterday and today*, 1948.

McPhail, Helen *Wilfred Owen, Poet and Soldier*, 1993.

Maund, T.E. *Birkenhead Transport*, 1959.

Mortimer, William Williams *History of Wirral*, 1847.

Neilsen, Harry E. *Auld-Lang-Syne*, 1935.

Newspaper Cuttings Collection, Central Information Service, Birkenhead Library.

Orchard, B. Guinness *Liverpool's Legion of Honour*, 1897.

Ordnance Survey *Map of Cheshire, 25 to 1*, 1875.

Pevsner, Niklaus and Edward Hubbard *The Buildings of England, Cheshire*, 1971.

Photographic Archive Central Information Service, Birkenhead Library.

Reilly, Charles and Aslan *Outline plan for the Borough of Birkenhead*, 1947.

Smith, Wilfred, F.J. Monkhouse and H.R. Wilkinson, editors *A Scientific Survey of Merseyside*, 1953.

Victory Souvenir of The Great War 1914-1919, Birkenhead News.

Stewart-Brown, R. *Birkenhead and the Mersey Ferry*, 1925.

Sulley, Philip *History of Ancient and Modern Birkenhead*, 1907.

Sulley, Philip *Hundred of Wirral*, 1907.

Thompson, F.H. *Roman Cheshire*, 1965.

Varley, W.J. *Cheshire Before the Romans*, 1964.

Woods, E. Cuthbert and P. Culverwell Brown *Rise and Progress of Wallasey*, 1929.

INDEX

Abbotsford Red Cross Hospital 101
Abernathy, James 46
Adair, Red 166
Air Raid Precautions Committee 124
Albert Memorial Industrial School 40,
    61, 91, 107, 138
Albert, Prince Consort 60
Albion Hotel 54
Albion Street 80
Alfred Dock 55, 123
Allanson, John 77
Allansons 77
Allen, Chesney 127
Allerton, R. 92
Altrincham 104
Alwen Gravitation Scheme 73
Alwen Reservoir 110
Alwen River 73
Alwen Street 80
American Civil War 65
Amstel 94
Anderson 125
Argyle Music Hall 45, 51-3, 57, 81-6,
    92, 94, 106, 108, 120, 126-8, 150,
    157
Argyle Street 52, 81, 85-86, 94, 106,
    120, 127
Argylle Street South 126
Ark Royal 120, 123, 128, 137
Arkle, Alderman 107
Arkle, Mr A.H. 87
Arkle, Mrs A.H. 99
Arkle, Mrs A.K. 94
Armistice Day 108
Arnold, Matthew 37
ARP 130
Arrowe 87, 101, 110, 112-13, 116,
    158
Arrowe Hall 87, 101, 110, 112
Arrowe Park 87, 112-13, 116, 158
Arrowe Park Hospital 87, 158
Arrowsmith, Randle 26

Art Gallery 104, 106, 113-15, 123, 142,
    151, 157
Arthur, H.G. 142
Arts Centre 115
ASLEF 152
Asquith, Prime Minister 94
Assembly Rooms 54, 158
Associated Society of Locomotive
    Engineers 152
Astaire, Fred 143
Aston Villa 150
Atkin, George 73
Attlee, Clement 131
Augmentation Court 26
Austin, Samuel 123
Baden-Powell, Robert Stephenson Smyth
    86, 112
Bantam Battalion 94
Bantam Volunteers 101
Barbour, Nicholas 20
Barrow 156
Bartley, Jack 148
Barton, Thomas 27
Baxter 148
Baylee, Dr Joseph 55, 58
Beaconsfield, Lord 29
Beaumont 69
Bebington 37, 68, 76, 83, 94, 152
Bebington Road 76, 94
Becheton, John 20, 22
Beckwith Street 72
Beechcroft 138
Beechcroft Educational Settlement 138
Beechwood Estate 165
Belgian Relief Fund 94
Belgrano 73, 156
Bell, Harold 151
Bell, Robert Charles 'Bunny' 150
Benedictine Order 15
Bentinck Street 73
Bentley Brothers 78
'Berstyered' 11

Bidston 22, 41, 54, 91, 96, 110-11, 151, 153, 157, 163

Bidston Court 153, 157

Bidston Dock 110

Bidston Hill 91, 163

Bidston Manor 91, 110

Bierce Heved 14-15

Bigland, Mr A.H. 109

Binns, Revd William 72

Birkenhead Borough Hospital 46, 52, 64, 100, 105

Birkenhead Docks 30, 32, 36, 44, 46, 55, 133

Birkenhead Hall 27, 99

Birkenhead High School 73

Birkenhead News 31, 91, 95, 100-1, 105-6, 108

Birkenhead Park 32-3, 35, 39, 41, 48-52, 61, 63, 74, 76, 81, 91, 104, 108, 113, 120, 145, 148-9, 157-8, 166

Birkenhead Priory 15-18, 20, 24-7, 33, 72, 166

Bismarck 128

Black Death 23

Black Monks 18

Blair, Tony 153

Blitz 57, 126-9, 134, 140, 148

Blood, Lieutenant-Colonel F.W. 75-76

Boer War 75, 98, 137

Boht, Bill 143

Boht, Jean 143

Bolton 72

Bootle Docks 55

Bowdon 25

Bowers, John 78, 115

Brassey, Thomas 30, 46, 60

Bridewell 58, 99

Bridge Street 14, 75, 117, 160

British Restaurants 124

Brittain, T.A. 134

Brodie, J.A. 111

Bromborough 22, 136

Bromborough Power Station 136

Brown, Ford Madox 114

Bruce, Albert 37

Brunlees 71

Bryanston Road 120

Budden, Lionel 37, 112

Bulley, Mrs Raffles 92

Bunny, Ernest Henry 125

Burgess, Inspector 58

Burns, Robbie 163

Butler, Sir Richard H.K 112

Byrkehed, Forest of 21

Byrne Avenue 54, 145

Callaghan, James 153

Cammell, Charles 87

Cammell Laird 37, 87, 90, 106-7, 123, 128-9, 137, 155-6, 160, 163

Canada Works 60

Carleton Players 158

Carlton Players 127

Carnegie, Andrew 111

Carney, Kate 84

Carter, Howard 111

Castle, Barbara 142-3

Cathcart Street Baptist Church 54

Catley, Gwen 143

Cavell, Edith 100, 105

Chamberlain, Prime Minister Neville 124

Chancellor, Lord 109

Charing Cross 76, 78, 83

Charity Committee 106

Charles I 27

Chatsworth House 33

Cheshire Greys 75

Cheshire Regiment 90, 94, 141

Cheshire Volunteer Rifles 58

Cheshire Volunteers 63

Chester 15, 20-1, 23, 26-7, 32, 34, 44, 58-9, 69, 72, 86, 88, 96, 98, 104, 108, 137, 142, 156, 160

Chester, Abbot of 23

Chester, Richard 26

Chester Castle 20, 23, 58

Chester Museum 98

Chester Road 96, 104, 156

Chester Street 27, 34, 86, 88, 137

Chester Street Mission Sunday School 137

Child Poverty Action Group 153

Church of Our Lady 126

Church Street 75, 125

Churchill, Winston 94, 129-30

Clarke, Dennis J. 53, 81, 84, 92, 127

Clarke, Mr Tom 125

Claughton 21-2, 33, 45, 52, 54, 59, 66, 78, 110
Claughton Circle 110
Claughton Manor 33, 59
Claughton Road 52, 54, 66
Claughton Road Music Hall 54, 66
Cleveland, John 27
Cleveland, William, Junior 27
Cleveland Street 81
Clevelands 27
Clifton Road Congregational Church 54
Clifton Ward 148
Clough, Brian 151
Coalition Unionists 109
Cochrane, J. 163
Cohen, Lord 140, 144
Cohen, Sir Henry 73, 144
Cole, Edith 52, 81
Cole Street 80-1
Coles, J. Ian 142-3
Collick, Percy 131, 144, 152-3
Colquhoun, Robin S. 143
Communal Feeding Committee 124
Concert Hall 54, 158
Connaught, Duke of 116
Conway Park 160
Conway Street 40, 76, 85, 120, 127, 143, 160, 167
Cooper, Anthony Ashley 137
Corporation Road 60, 126
Cotman, John Sell 113
County Courts 22
Cox, David 113
Cox, Edward 113
Craven Rooms 54
Crimean War 60
Cripps, Sir Stafford 121
Cromie, Robert FRIBA 128
CSS *Alabama* 65
Cunningham, John 112
Cust, Lady 54
Cust, Sir Edward 58
Daily Arrowe 116
Dallow, Canon 97
Dallow, Very Revd Wilfred Canon 97
Daniels, Bebe 143
Darwen 81
Dashley, Charles 96

Davis, William 123
Deakin, Thomas 73
Dean, William Ralph 'Dixie' 120, 150
Delcy, Miss 54
Dell, Edmund 153
Della Robbia 77-8, 96, 112, 114-15
Denbigh 27
Derby, Earl of 110-11, 116
Derby, Lord 91, 97, 123
Derby County 151
Devonshire, Duke of 33
Disraeli, Benjamin 29
Dobson, John 129
Dock Cottages 59, 122
Dock Road 163
Dock Scheme 46, 54, 74
Dock Strikes 125, 127
Dodd, Miss Hilda 106
Dover 114
Downing Street 121
Dramatic Society 127
Dressler 115
Drill Hall 75, 96
Drury Lane 54
Duke of Edinburgh Award Scheme 145
Dunblane 21
Dundee 81
Durban 81
Durham City 150
Dyserth Holiday Camp 121
Eastham 23
Eccles 26
Edinburgh 29, 35
Edinburgh, Duke of 141, 145, 158
Edith Cavell Memorial Ward 100, 105
Education Act 1870, 72
Edward I 20-1, 38, 72
Edward III 21, 26
Edward VII 69, 75, 85, 87, 142
Edwards, Mr Frank 148
Egerton 73, 80, 107, 162
Egerton Dock 162
Egerton Street 80
Eisteddfod, Young Men's 54
Eisteddfod Gadeiriol 54
Eldon Gardens 144, 154, 165
Elizabeth, Queen 129, 137-8, 144
Elizabeth II 141, 158

Ellesmere Port 160
Ellison, C.O. 38, 71, 159
English Civil War 27
Enrica 65
Escheator 27
Essoldo Cinemas 143
Europa Park 158, 165
Europa Pool 160
Europe Day 130
EuroWirral 159-60
Evans, Mrs 92
Everton 120, 150-1
Exmouth Street 76, 141
Ferdinand, Archduke Franz 94
Field, Frank 11, 153
Fields, Gracie 127, 167
Flanagan, Bud 127
Flaybrick Hill 41, 59
Fleming, Horace 138
Ford Estate 165
Ford Hill 165
Forde, Florrie 84, 127
Formby, George, Junior 84
Formby, George, Senior 84
Frankby 153, 157
Frater 16
Friars, Austin 24
Fyfe, Sir David Maxwell 140
Galicia 95
Gamlin, Lionel 143
Gamon, Gilbert P. 38, 72
Garibaldi, Guiseppe 55
Gatehouse, Charles 96, 112
Gaumont 128
General Election 107, 109, 131, 152-3
General Strike 109, 120
George V 87, 90, 98, 106-7, 111, 115
George VI 129
Gill, Alfred 67
Gillespie 29, 32, 34-5, 37, 39, 55, 59,
    76, 132, 160
Girtin, Thomas 113
Gitana, Gertie 84
Gitana Ladies Choir 54
Glenda Jackson Theatre 144, 157
Gloucester Art School 113
Golden Arrow 117
Goldsmith, Edward 77

Goodison Park 150
Gorsedd 104
Gostenhofer, Mrs 97
Goulding, Father 58
Graham, James Gillespie 29, 32, 34-5
Gramell, Dennis 53
Grange Hotel 78, 83
Grange Lane 45, 58, 77
Grange Road 52, 54, 62, 71, 75-8, 83,
    85-6, 108, 112, 120, 127, 131-2, 143,
    145, 158-60
Grange Road West 75, 127, 143, 145,
    158
Gray, Evans and Crossley 111
Grayson, H.M. 109
Greenock 27, 37
Gretna Green 28
Griffith, Ellis J. 107
Griffiths, Mr 96
Griffiths, Mrs Stanley 145
Grimsby 116
Hadley 81
Hamilton Quarter 37, 160
Hamilton Square 28, 35-9, 43, 45, 59,
    67, 70-1, 77-8, 81, 85, 108, 112, 114,
    117, 120, 130-1, 134, 140-1, 144,
    160, 164
Hamilton Street 51, 111, 113
Hampton House 53, 63
Hance, Ian 151
Hancourt 109
Harlow, Jean 128
Harrison, Albert 77
Hartley, Henry 38, 72, 93
Hartley, Jesse 162
Hatteras 66
Healey, Mrs Edna 156
Hemingford Road 101
Hemingford Road School Hospital 101
Hemingford Street 64, 108
Henderson 55, 159
Henry VIII 25-6
Heswall 152
Higher Bebington 83
Hillbark 157
Hillbark Players 157
Hinton, Richard 142
Hitler, Adolf 124

HMS Ajax 154
HMS Ark Royal 120, 123, 137
HMS Audacious 87
HMS Bronington 163
HMS Conqueror 156
HMS Devonshire 154
HMS Exmouth 66, 87
HMS Glory 66
HMS Hampshire 98
HMS Onyx 163, 167
HMS Panther 87
HMS Plymouth 163, 167
HMS Prince of Wales 123, 129
HMS Renown 156
HMS Repulse 129
HMS Revenge 156
HMS Rodney 107, 123
HMS Saracen 129
HMS Thetis 123
HMS Thrasher 86
HMS Thunderbolt 124
HMS Unicorn 156
HMS Wolf 87
Hobson, Valerie 143
Holden, Cecil 145
Holt, Alfred 106, 112
Holt, Ian 152
Holt Technical School 138
Holy Trinity Church 55, 58
Horlick, Nicola 73
Hornblower, Lewis 52
Howarth, Simon 151
Howell, Dennis 149
Hoylake 14, 152
Hubbard, Edward 37
Hudson, Robert 157
Hull 65
Huskisson Dock 126
Hutchinson, Leslie 143
Hutchinson, Miss Phyllis 96
Hyne, Hugh 25
International Jazz Guitar Festival 158
Jackson, Geoffrey 32
Jackson, William 32-3, 40, 43, 59-60, 72, 138
Jagger, David 116
Jeffs, Revd Rob 64
John, King 15, 20

Johnson, Peter 149
Johnson, Robert White 154
Johnston, Robert Edward 69
Joyce, William 125
Keegan, Alderman Miss Eileen M. 151
Kelly, W.W. 52, 62, 81, 85, 104, 127
Kemp, John 113
Kennedy, Jacqueline 121
Kent, Duchess of 145
King, Hetty 84, 127
Kirby, Edmund 37
Kister, Misses 28
Kitchener, Lord 98-9
Knox, Canon Andrew 66, 97
Knox, Revd Andrew 72
Labour Exchange 117
Laird, Captain Gordon 75
Laird, Jessie 32
Laird, John 27, 37, 43, 46, 55, 61, 63-4, 66-7, 72, 75, 138
Laird, John, Junior 27, 63, 67
Laird, John, Senior 66, 75
Laird, MacGregor 153, 157
Laird, Miss Annie 107
Laird, William 26, 28-9, 32, 37, 40, 43, 61, 137, 159
Laird, William, Junior 137
Laird School of Art 138
Laird Shipyards 44, 65
Lamorna Cove 113
Landican 110
Lang, C.E. 59
Lauder, Harry 83
Lawton 32
Lea, Richard 163
Leasowe Castle 54
Lee, Arthur H. 115, 121
Leicester City 150
Lever, William Hesketh 64, 92
Leverhulme, Lord 110, 112
Library Service 46, 111, 142
Lichfield 25
Liverpool 15, 22-3, 26-30, 32, 35, 53, 55, 64-5, 69, 71, 73, 83, 94, 106, 108, 110-12, 114, 123, 125-6, 131, 136, 138, 143, 151, 158
Liverpool Bay 123
Liverpool City Mission 64

Liverpool Daily Post 108
Liverpool University 73, 131, 138
Livingstone, Dr David 29, 43, 73
Llewellyn, Prince of Gwynedd 21
Lloyd George, Prime Minister David
    105, 109
Locke, Harold 148
Low Water Basin 55
Lowry, Mrs 64
Lowry, Wilfred 148
Lucan, Arthur 84
Lyon, Ben 143
MacDonald, Prime Minister Ramsay 121
MacIver, Mr David 107
Mallory, George 72
Manor Road 115
Manzoni 115
Mappa Mundi 15
Market Hall 35, 55
Market Street 46, 67, 76, 94, 160
Martin, Mrs 96
Masaniello 112
Mason, Edward George 115
Massey, Mr May 101
Masterton, Valerie 158
Mathias, Ray 150
McCann, Michael 77
McFarland, Roy 151
McGaul, Alderman James H. 148
McLeod, Mr 96
Memorial Church 115
Meols 14
Mercer, Mrs Mary Anne 151
Merritt, Mayor Mr James 106
Mersey Docks 35, 46, 55
Mersey Joint Tunnel Committee 111
Mersey Park 71, 107
Mersey Park Military Hospital 107
Mersey Railway Tunnel 69
Mersey Road School 72
Mersey Tunnel 110, 117, 119-20, 132,
    142, 145
Middle Ages 26
Milnes, G.F. 80-1
Mitty, James 77
Moody, Captain A.R. 131
Moreton 109
Morpeth, Lord 38

Morris, William 114
Motte, Sir Basil 111
Mrs Miniver 127
Music Hall 52, 54, 66, 81
National Savings 130
National War Savings Committee 106
Nore, William 22
Norman, Richard 24
Norton Priory 26
O'Shea, Kitty 84
Oakshott, Tom 73
Oates, Alderman Jack 144
Old Chester Road 96, 104
Oldham Athletic 150
Oliver Street 53, 63
Operatic Society 127
Orderly Avenue 80
Orderly Place 80
Ostermann, Bruce 149
Ould, Edward 157
Overchurch Runic Stones 98
Owen, Wilfred 73, 108-9, 167
Oxton 45, 59, 64-5, 68, 73, 76-8, 84,
    94, 96-7, 107, 110, 129, 138
Oxton Congregational Church 64
Oxton Road 76-7, 84, 96-7, 129, 138
Oxton Road Adult School 138
Pacific Road 162
Paco Peña 158
Palm Grove 80, 101
Park Cricket Club 145
Paxton, Joseph 33, 41, 49, 55
Paynter, Mr Charles Edwin 96
Peck, Gregory 143
Peggy Machree 85
Penn, W.C. 113
Pevsner, Nikolaus 69
Philharmonic Society 54
Pilgrim Street 97
Platt, Alderman Hugh 143
Polaris Submarine Project 154, 156
Poole, Randle 26
Poor Law Administration 92
Poor Law Amendment Act 63
Portland Stone 111, 128
Pott, Walter 86
Powell, Sir Thomas 27
Prenton 59, 76, 78, 110, 125, 134, 138

Prenton Park 149, 151

Price, Francis 27-29 32, 46

Price, Richard Parry 28

Price Street 38, 46, 58, 64, 120, 140, 142

Proctor, C.J. 85

Proctor, Riflemen A.H. 106

Public Baths 54, 73

Public Libraries Act 1850 46, 72

Pyke, William 77

Queen Mary 90, 92, 106, 116

Queen Victoria 37-38, 40, 75, 77, 115

Rainford, Thomas 24-5

Rampling, R.B. 35

Randle, J.M. 55

Rathbone, Harold 78, 114

Ray, Ted 127

Rayneford, Thomas 25

Reader, Ralph 158

Reilly, Professor Sir Charles 132, 140

Rendel, James Meadows 33, 35, 46, 111, 162

Rendel Street 111

Resurgam 162

Reynforth, Thomas 24

Richard III 52

River Birket 14

River Mersey 131

RMS Lusitania 96

RMS Fullagar 123

RSM Mauritania 123

RMS Queen Mary 121

RMS Strathmore 121

Robbia, Luca Della 115

Rock Ferry 46, 65, 72-3, 76, 109

Roget, Pascal 158

Romer, Anne 54

Roodee 142

Roosevelt, President 129

Rose Marie 127

Rostances 104, 159

Routledge, Patricia 73, 158

Rowlands, Mr D.R. 108

Rowse, Herbert J. 111, 132, 136

Rowton Moor 27

Royal Rock Ferry 65

Royden Park 157

Ryder, Miss Helen 107

Saintogne 26

Sale 148

Sandiway 94

Saronie, M. 77

Shackleton, Mr 91

Shaftesbury, Earl of 137

Shaftesbury Boys 137, 144

Shakespeare, William 37, 112

Shankar, Ravi 158

Sharpe, Prior John 25-6

Shaw, George Bernard 104

Shaw, John Ralph 112

Sheffield 81, 87

Shepherd, John 142

Shoreham 114

Shrewsbury 65, 108

Shrewsbury, Earl of 65

Sidney Street 111

Singer Sewing Machine Co 77

Smith, F.E. 72, 91, 94, 107, 127

Smith, H. Tyson 37, 112

Smith, Harold 127

Soskice, Frank 131

Stanley Road 115

Starr, Freddie 11

Steer, P Wilson 113

Stephenson, George 32, 44

Stoke City 149

Stratton, George 114, 142

Stubbs, George 123

Sudla Bay 129

Sulley 46, 168

Swarb, John 96

Tallon, Canon 126

Tarver, Canon 69

Taylor, Robert 127

Taylor Street 80, 111

Telford, Thomas 33

Temple Road 101

Theatre Metropole 52

Theatre Royal 52, 54, 81, 85, 104, 106, 127, 157

Thingwall 110

Thompson, Annie 64, 72, 108

Thompson, Charles 64-5, 72, 97, 108, 144

Thurstaston 71

Tiddesbury, Prior Roger de 22

Tobin, Sir John 30

Town Hall 21, 28, 35, 37-8, 54, 70-2, 75, 79, 90, 93-94, 99, 130, 151, 156-8, 160

Train, George Francis 35-6, 39, 160

Tranmere Rovers Football Club 104, 120, 148-52

Tutty, Fred 77

Tyler, Wat 23

Upton 91, 97, 110, 165

Upton Road 91

Vacher, Dr Francis 74

Verne, Jules 35, 39

Vernon, Richard de 22

Victoria Park 71, 85, 100

Voss, Milnes and Co. 80-1

Vyner, Lord 91

Wales, Prince of 69, 75, 85, 112, 116, 123, 129, 163

Wales, Princess of 115

Wales, Royal National Eisteddfod of 104

Walker, Cassandia Anne 115

Walker Art Gallery 114

Wallasey 28, 30, 33, 38, 74, 94, 113, 115, 148, 152, 165, 167

Wallasey Pool 28, 30, 33, 74, 113

Walley, Henry de 22

Walton 91

Waring, Pongo 150

Waterford Street 97

Watson Street 96

Webb, Beatrice 92

Westminster, Duke of 71

Westminster, Marquis of 52

Westminster Abbey 37

Whetstone Lane 81, 138, 141, 145

White, H. Graham 72, 95, 107, 109, 131, 138

Wilkins, Liz 115

Willaston 21

Williamson, John 61, 104, 113

Williamson Art Gallery 104, 106, 115, 123, 142, 151, 157

Willmer, Miss J.H. 91

Wilson, Harold Sir 121, 153

Wint, Peter de 113

Wirral 15, 21-22, 26, 35, 37-8, 64, 143-4, 148, 151-2, 156, 158-60, 165

Wirral Forest 21

Wirral Museum 37, 156, 160

Wirral Museums 158

Wirral Railway 158

Wolverhampton 139, 159

Woodchurch 71, 110, 130, 132, 134-7, 143, 145

Woodchurch Road 71, 130

Woodcroft 96

Woodside Ferry 32, 39, 67, 69, 82, 121, 140, 162-3

Woodside Ferry Approach 68, 163

Woodward, Miss Elsie 100

World War One 72-3, 81, 91, 94, 100, 108, 112, 124, 140, 167

World War Two 59, 122, 124, 126, 130, 142, 149

Worrall, Mr 108

Worsley, Ralph 26

WRVS 130

WVS 126

Wyatt, M.J. 156

YMCA 54, 85-6, 112, 144-5

Zeigler, Mr J.H. 91

Zeigler, Mrs 91